Responding to Constraint

Other titles recently published under the SRHE/OU Press imprint:

Michael Allan: *The Goals of Universities*
William Birch: *The Challenge to Higher Education*
Heather Eggins: *Restructuring Higher Education*
Colin Evans: *Language People*
Gunnar Handal and Per Lauvås: *Promoting Reflective Teaching*
Vivien Hodgson *et al.*: *Beyond Distance Teaching, Towards Open Learning*
Peter Linklater: *Education and the World of Work*
Graeme Moodie: *Standards and Criteria in Higher Education*
John Pratt and Suzanne Silverman: *Responding to Constraint*
Majorie E. Reeves: *The Crisis in Higher Education*
John T. E. Richardson *et al.*: *Student Learning*
Derek Robbins: *The Rise of Independent Study*
Gordon Taylor *et al.*: Literacy by Degrees
Alan Woodley *et al.*: *Choosing to Learn*

Responding to Constraint

Policy and Management in
Higher Education

John Pratt and
Suzanne Silverman

The Society for Research into Higher Education
& Open University Press

Published by SRHE and
Open University Press
Open University Educational Enterprises Limited
12 Cofferidge Close
Stony Stratford
Milton Keynes MK11 1BY

and
242 Cherry Street
Philadelphia, PA 19106, USA

First Published 1988

British Library Cataloguing in Publication Data

Pratt, John, *1945–*
    Responding to constraint policy and
    management in higher education.
    1. Great Britain. Higher education. Policies
    of government
    I. Title   II. Silverman, Suzanne
    379.41

ISBN 0-335-09500-3

Library of Congress Cataloging-in-Publication Data

Pratt, John.
    Responding to constraint : policy and management in higher
    education / John Pratt and Suzanne Silverman.
        p.   cm.
    Includes index.
    ISBN 0-335-09500-3
    1. Community colleges – England – Administration – Case studies.
    2. Technical institutes – England – Administration – Case studies.
    3. Community colleges – England – Business management – Case studies.
    4. Technical institutes – England – Business management – Case studies.
    5. Federal aid to higher education – England – Case studies.
    6. Strategic planning – England – Case studies.   I. Silverman.
    Suzanne Jo, 1950–   .   II. Title.
    LB2341.8.G7P73   1988
    378.42 – dc19   88-9893 CIP

Typeset by Rowland Phototypesetting Limited, Bury St Edmunds, Suffolk
Printed in Great Britain by
St Edmundsbury Press Limited, Bury St Edmunds, Suffolk

To Irving and Claire Silverman
who made it possible

Contents

Preface

This book is the result of a number of (mainly) happy accidents, and of the efforts of many people. The research project on which it is based developed from a meeting on another topic between Leslie Wagner, then Deputy Secretary at the National Advisory Body for Public Sector Higher Education, Gerry Fowler, Director of North East London Polytechnic, John Davies, then Head of Department in the Anglian Regional Management Centre at NELP and me. The idea of monitoring the NAB planning exercise was developed into a research proposal by John Davies and me and submitted to the Department of Education and Science. At the Department's request, it was combined with a related proposal by John Gill from Sheffield City Polytechnic and the resulting joint project was funded by the Department with a grant eventually totalling some £139 000. We would like to record here our recognition and thanks to John Davies for the essential contribution he made in the design and successful negotiation of the project with the DES.

The study itself could not have been completed without the contribution of many people. First we would mention the directors, staff and students of the case study institutions, who gave freely of their time and their views. We greatly appreciate their frankness, even when on occasion it was directed against us, and we have tried to respect the confidentiality of what were often critical and sometimes delightfully indiscreet observations on their experiences. Because of this, we cannot mention their names, and whilst they and we know who they are, we hope not too many others will.

The project was guided by a Steering Group established by the DES and whilst once or twice we found its requirements irksome, it made a major contribution to the direction and structure of the study and we enjoyed the exchange of views that it promoted. The Steering Group was initially chaired by David Forrester, then Assistant Secretary at the DES, whose drive and strong views we gradually learned to respect and admire, and we were sorry he had to move on to higher things elsewhere. His duties were taken over by Michael Smith. Other members were: Dr C. Booth – DES (HMI); Dr R. Cowell – Sunderland Polytechnic; Mr R. S. Johnson – Director of Education (Leeds); Mr S. Lapointe – OECD; Mr R. Leeson – Ealing College of Higher Education; Dr J. May and Mr T. Easingwood – Derbyshire College of Higher Education;

Professor J. Morris – Manchester Business School; Professor J. Sizer – Loughborough University; Mr L. Wagner – NAB and Mr J. Wyatt – West Sussex Institute of Higher Education.

The outcome of the research project was a series of eight case studies of individual institutions and a final report to the Department. These works are Crown Copyright (1987) and were produced under contract with the Department of Education and Science. The views expressed are those of the authors and do not necessarily reflect those of the DES or any other Government Department. Copies of these works have been circulated by the Department to a limited audience. This book is based on some of the material in them, but also includes new material. The two research teams divided topics of study between them and each was also responsible for four case studies. This book is based only on the topics studied by the team at North East London Polytechnic, though it draws on the case studies of all eight institutions, and we would thus wish to acknowledge the contribution of John Gill and his research team.

There are few activities that are not improved by the comments and criticisms of others. We have been particularly fortunate at the Centre for Institutional Studies in having numerous colleagues who have made contributions of this kind. Not least is Michael Locke, Senior Research Fellow, who not only co-wrote one chapter of this book, but offered support, information, and sage criticism throughout. An enormous amount of work and a stimulating variety of ideas were contributed by Rory O'Hara, who was research assistant for the project and who in particular contributed the bulk of the material on which Chapters 3 and 6 are based. As we note in Chapter 4, a major research project of this kind is as much an administrative as an intellectual challenge. We could not have maintained the level of output required by the DES nor the timetable without the help of Linda Harris, our project research administrator, nor without the advice from Patrick Hare on word processing.

As always, whilst each of these people made a contribution to the study, none can be held responsible for the outcome or for any of the views expressed in this book. But it would not have been the same without them.

John Pratt
Great Neck, New York 1988

1

Analysing the Impact of Public Policy: The Theoretical Background

On 26 July 1982, all institutions in England receiving funds from the Advanced Further Education (AFE) Pool, and their maintaining authorities, received a letter from the National Advisory Body for Local Authority Higher Education (as it then was) advising them of a planning exercise to be conducted for the allocation of AFE Pool funds in 1984–5. The creation of the National Advisory Body (NAB) in 1982 and the implementation of its first planning exercise in 1984–5 represented a major change in government education policy. A new organization was set up to determine the distribution of funding and student places to colleges and polytechnics and carry out government policy through its control of the distributive mechanism. What was the impact of this policy on higher education institutions?

This was the major question addressed by a 2-year research study of the responses of eight institutions – four polytechnics and four colleges – commissioned by the Secretary of State for Education and Science in September 1983. The study, which began in November 1983, was conducted by two research teams at the Department of Management Studies, Sheffield City Polytechnic and the Centre for Institutional Studies, North East London Polytechnic. It explored the organization structures, management styles and strategic planning and review processes in institutions as they responded to constraint, to attempt to identify characteristics which influenced their responses; their adaptability; their management and planning processes and the ways in which they set priorities and the factors influencing these processes; the effects of financial constraint on these structures and processes. The study was focused on the NAB planning exercise, though it was recognized that this was part of a continuing period of restraint, many of the outcomes of which indeed lay outside the time-scale of the project.

The study had two major outcomes. The first was detailed case studies of the eight institutions. Copies of these are available on request from the research teams. Second was an overall report to the Secretary of State analysing the case material and summarizing the main findings of the research teams. A limited number of copies has been circulated by the Department of Education and Science (DES). This book is based on the material collected and analysed in the case studies and the final report, but it concentrates on, and takes further, the analyses of the research team at the Centre for Institutional Studies, North East London Polytechnic. Its particular concern is the impact of policy on higher education institutions and how they responded to the constraints and opportunities which they faced in this period of financial constraint. It examines the institutional strategies developed and the institutions' mechanisms of resource allocation and control, academic development and planning, and the effect of external constraints on the way in which national policies or processes impact upon institutions, and of the factors conditioning the way that institutions respond to them.

This book thus differs from many studies by seeking to examine the managerial responses of institutions, not just in managerial terms, but also as consequences of policy. Existing literature in business studies, management and public administration does of course deal generally with the problems and effects of financial constraint. It points to the importance of such issues as the organizational characteristics enhancing adaptability, coping strategies, the need for strategic planning, criteria for choice, and similar factors that need to be taken into account in institutions facing constraint.

Little of this literature, however, addresses questions of policy and its implementation. Much of it, moreover, concerns the private sector, and there is in particular little specific research into the effect of financial policy on higher educational institutions. Davies and Morgan (1982) and Shattock and Rigby (1983) were the only substantial studies into financial constraint in higher education in Britain at the time this study commenced. Equally, most studies on higher education policy, administration and management are, because of the recent speed of change in the system, historic, dealing with outdated policies and circumstances. There have been few opportunities to study the new arrangements in public sector higher education. Knight (1981) and Pratt (1982) are perhaps the only recent detailed scrutinies of NAB funding arrangements. This was the first large-scale study of the effects of an entirely new departure in planning and funding in the public sector, and offered detailed accounts of the responses of individual institutions to a national planning exercise, as well as identifying the factors which affected institutions both differently and similarly and which conditioned their responses.

How do we assess the impact of the NAB exercise and analyse the implementation of this change in government policy? When we examine the literature on policy analysis, we find that recent studies have moved away from a narrow concern with the decision-making process and stress the importance of the implementation of policy. Earlier studies assumed that implementation would follow automatically from policy decisions, but since the publication of Pressman and Wildavsky's study of implementation in 1973, interest in this aspect of the policy process has grown. One reason for this interest was a need to understand policy 'failure', which was seen as the outcome of many ambitious new programmes adopted by governments in the 1960s to deal with complex social problems. Quade (1982), for example, writing of the United States' experience, records that: '. . . solutions have often been promised, but when they have been tried out, they have been disappointing at best and frequently seemed to worsen the situation' and that 'dissatisfaction with the results of the decision making processes in use by government is apparent' (p. 1). He argues for policy analysis to 'help public decision-makers make better choices' (p. 13).

The concept of policy 'failure' takes policy as the starting point and assumes that there are problems which prevent a particular policy from being implemented successfully. It draws a firm line between the decision-making process, whose outcome is a particular policy, and the implementation process, whose outcome is seen as the success or failure of the policy.

This view of implementation can be related to earlier theories of policy analysis which set up ideal-type models of 'rational' policy-making and attempted to define the necessary conditions for such a process to take place. Simon is perhaps the most well-known author of the 'ideal type' model in his seminal books in the 1940s and 1950s (Simon 1947, 1957a, b). Lindblom (1959) defines the elements of rational policy-making in terms of the identification of values, leading to the specification of objectives, options for achieving these objectives and finally the choice of which options would maximize the values earlier defined as being the most important. Lindblom then goes on to show that actual policy-makers are unlikely to follow this ideal-type process and that, in fact, 'muddling through' is a far better description of reality. Simon (1960) too discusses the limits to rationality in real-life policy-making. Simon, however, believed that policy-makers could move toward more 'rational' policy-making through the use of the 'new science of management decision'. His view is, at least to some extent, supported by Dror (1968, 1971), who argues for an 'economically rational model' in which rational analysis in decision-making is pursued as far as, but only as far as, the benefit outweighs the cost. Somewhere between the two views also lies Etzioni (1967) arguing for 'mixed scanning' with detailed analysis of some areas of policy but not others.

Much of the literature on policy analysis thus accepts an ideal-type model of rational policy-making. Such an approach assumes that policy is a set of objectives which may not be carried out in practice because of various limitations. Implementation is then concerned with the preconditions which would have to be achieved in order to put policy into practice. Hogwood and Gunn (1984, pp. 199–206) identify eight preconditions for 'perfect implementation': the circumstances external to the implementing agency do not impose crippling constraints; that adequate time and sufficient resources are made available to the programme; that the required combination of resources is actually available; that the policy to be implemented is based upon a valid theory of cause and effect; that there is understanding of, and agreement on, objectives; that tasks are fully specified in correct sequence; that there is perfect communication and coordination; and that those in authority can demand and obtain perfect compliance.

A crucial aspect of this ideal-type model is that it assumes that the policies to be implemented are a rational means for achieving the goals of policy-makers, or 'that the policy is based on a valid theory of cause and effect'. If this is not the case, policy failure can be the outcome. Numerous authors have identified ways in which these failures of implementation arise. Allison (1971), for example, showed how different people's 'conceptual lenses' lead to different interpretations of events and hence different outcomes. Dror (1986), in characterizing 'policy making' under adversity, shows how governments react irrationally to adverse circumstances.

When discussing the outcomes of the policy process, Hogwood and Gunn distinguish between what they call 'non-implementation' and 'unsuccessful implementation'. In the former, a policy is not put into effect as intended, whereas unsuccessful implementation occurs when a policy is carried out in full, but this fails to produce the intended results (or outcomes). In the case where a policy was based on inadequate information, defective reasoning or unrealistic assumptions, the cause of the failure can be attributed to 'bad policy' (Hogwood and Gunn 1984, p. 197).

One problem with starting with an ideal-type model, however, is that what might be seen as 'bad policy' from the point of view of top policy-makers might be regarded as an excellent compromise or successful 'result' from another point of view. In practice, policy is rarely a clear or fixed set of objectives which come out of the policy-making, as opposed to the implementation, process. In fact, as Barrett and Fudge (1981) point out in their criticism of what they see as the 'checklist' approach generated by the ideal-type model, implementation is not necessarily a logical step-by-step progression from policy intention to action. They criticize what they see as the 'top-down' or managerial approach to policy analysis:

> this perspective tends to be associated with hierarchical concepts of organisation; policy emanates from the 'top' (or centre) and is transmitted down the hierarchy (or to the periphery) and translated into more specific rules and procedures as it goes to guide or control action at the bottom (or on the ground). (Barrett and Fudge 1981, p. 12)

Barrett and Fudge question a number of assumptions which underlie this approach: that policy comes from the top and is the starting point for action, that all action relates to a specific or explicit policy, and that implementers are agents for policy-makers and, therefore, in a compliant relationship to policy-makers. They argue that in practice all of these assumptions may not hold and they present an alternative 'action-oriented' approach, which observes what actually happens or gets done and seeks to understand how and why:

> From this perspective, implementation (or action) may be regarded as a series of responses . . . this involves considering implementation in terms of power relations and different mechanisms for gaining or avoiding influence or control. (p. 13)

This approach prefers to see the policy–action relationship not as a linear progression over time but as a process of interaction and negotiation and emphasizes the environmental, political and organizational factors which influence implementation.

Hogwood and Gunn reject these criticisms of the top-down perspective. They maintain that Barrett and Fudge are creating a straw man and that at least some writers (including themselves) understand the interdependence of policy-making and implementation. While Hogwood and Gunn admit that, in practice, policy may be altered in the course of implementation, the ideal-type model starts with the assumption that policy is based on a valid theory of cause and effect and, therefore, changes in the course of implementation may be evidence of policy failure or bad policy. The logical next step in this kind of analysis is to see changes in policy in the course of implementation as bad practice.

> If pressed, we must plead guilty to a measure of sympathy with the top-down view, if only on the grounds that 'those seeking to put policy into effect' are usually elected while 'those upon whom action depends' are not, at least in the case of civil servants and the staff of health services, nationalised industries, etc. (Hogwood and Gunn 1984, p. 207)

They express concern with Barrett and Fudge's ready acceptance of, let alone their seeming acquiescence in, aspects of the policy–action continuum, particularly the tendency of lower-level actors to take decisions which effectively limit hierarchical influence, pre-empt top decision-making or alter policies. Hogwood and Gunn maintain that while implementation must involve a process of interaction between organizations, the members of which may have different values, perspective and priorities from one another and from those advocating the policy, much of this interaction can and should take place before policy formulation.

Without necessarily accepting that Barrett and Fudge do put any normative value on the 'bottom-up' aspects of the policy process, it is clear that Hogwood and Gunn dislike the alteration of policy in the course of implementation and would like to improve the effectiveness of implementation to prevent this form of bad practice from occurring. The problem with this kind of analysis, however, is that it tends to lose track of the important question, which is not whether the policy has been altered, but whether it accomplished what was intended in the first place. In Hogwood and Gunn's own terminology, unsuccessful implementation happens when policy fails to produce the intended results or outcomes. Is a policy which is completely altered in the course of implementation but succeeds in producing the intended results a 'worse' policy than one which is implemented in its original form but does the opposite of what was intended by policy-makers?

An approach which sees the outcomes of the policy process in terms of the impact of policy on a particular organization or society avoids the normative trap of putting any intrinsic value on either top-down or bottom-up implementation. Such an analysis can still be directed at improving policy implementation, but the prescriptive nature of such a model would come from its concern with how the policy actually worked out in practice rather than what happened to it in the course of implementation.

One way of avoiding the problems of the ideal-type model would be to take the policy-makers' intentions as a hypothesis to be tested. This kind of approach has been developed at the Centre for Institutional Studies (CIS) at North East London Polytechnic. It is based on some of the ideas of Sir Karl Popper (1960,

1966, 1975) and has proved useful in a number of studies of public policy in the UK and elsewhere. This approach is concerned with the problems which policies are designed to solve. It has the virtues of a 'rational' approach, in that it makes policies susceptible to rational analysis, but it also recognizes that various actors have different definitions of rationality. By analysing policies in terms of their success or failure in problem-solving, it allows researchers to assess the effectiveness of policies without accepting that what policy-makers do is necessarily 'rational'. This approach is thus able to deal with the conflicts or anarchy which are often involved in the implementation process. The CIS approach relies on Popper's formulation of the logic through which intellectual progress is made. His schema starts with the formulation of a problem for which a trial solution is proposed; the solution is then rigorously tested to eliminate error; and all of this leads to a new situation with new problems. The task of the scientist, whether social or natural, is thus one of trial and error, of inventing hypotheses which can be tested and submitting them to tests (Pratt, undated).

This approach takes policies as the hypotheses, as proposed solutions to particular problems, and this problem-solving approach proceeds by testing for error, in the way that science proceeds, and it offers us provisional knowledge. Policy is implemented through social institutions, and creating and running these institutions can be seen as a social technology. We have to ask of institutions, as we do of physical devices, whether they are fit for their purposes, whether they are achieving what is required of them. Again, the process is one of problem formulation, trial solution and testing. As a result, we can adjust the institution or use it differently.

One valuable aspect of the CIS approach is that it draws attention to the unintended consequences of public policy. As Popper pointed out, human action is not always consciously defined or explicable in terms of needs, hopes or motives: 'Even those which arise as the result of conscious and intended human actions are, as a rule, the indirect, the unintended and often unwanted by-products of such actions.' By starting with the problems which policies are trying to solve, this approach sees the impact of public policy as the outcome of the process, and this includes all the consequences, whether intended or not.

The policy-makers' intentions, however, remain central to the analysis, but this approach allows researchers to avoid some of the problems outlined by Barrett and Fudge. Even if a policy is not specific or explicit, researchers can look at the problem the policy was designed to solve and assess the situation in which the actors find themselves. In this kind of analysis we have found another of Popper's concepts to be useful. The idea of situational logic or situational analysis was developed by Popper in relation to historical explanation, but can be applied to public policy as well. Popper (1975, p. 179) writes in *Objective Knowledge*:

> By a situational analysis, I mean a certain kind of tentative or conjectural explanation of some human action which appeals to the situation in which the agent finds himself. . . . [We] can try, conjecturally, to give an idealised reconstruction of the *problem situation* in which the agent found himself, and to that extent make the action 'understandable' (or 'rationally understandable'), that is, adequate to his situation as he saw it.

This approach assumes that people will follow the logic of their situations and thus 'rationality' lies in people's problem-solving rather than in a model of 'perfect administration' which assumes that only the rationality of top policy-makers is at issue. The concept of situational logic has proved helpful in cases where government policies did not have a direct impact on institutions or where policies themselves were unclear. The task for researchers is to assess the constraints and opportunities within which institutions or actors are placed. The implication of the model for reformers or public administrators is that the potential for change in institutions consists not so much in issuing instructions as in setting up the situations, the logic of which will make desired outcomes more likely (Locke, undated).

Some of the advantages of this approach become clear when we put policy analysis in the context of a period of financial constraint. When there is an imperative to reduce expenditure, policy-makers often prefer to obscure the real intentions of their policies. Because the CIS approach takes stated policies as hypotheses and tests them in practice, it is not bound by the policy-makers' statements of their objectives, but views them sceptically, recognizing both that the expressed objectives may not be achieved and that other interpretations of the policies are possible and can be investigated.

The implementation of cuts in government programmes or services is such a political process that models of 'perfect administration' seem particularly inappropriate. It is not surprising that institutions facing cuts try to alter policies in the course of their implementation or that policy-makers prefer to avoid becoming identified with declining services. The concept of situational logic is helpful because it focuses on the institutions' assessment of their interests. Such an approach is consistent with Barrett and Fudge's understanding of the interaction between policy and action and the negotiations and political struggles which occur in the course of implementation. It does not assume that altering policies is in itself bad, because the outcome is more than a matter of whether cuts were actually made according to the intentions of the policy-makers. The central question is what were the impact of these cuts in the institutions?

When we use this approach to examine the NAB exercise and its impact on public sector higher education, we start with an analysis of the formal stated objectives of the exercise, but we are just as concerned with the informal negotiations between actors and with the changes which took place in the 'rules of the game'. We examine the logic of the situation in which higher education institutions found themselves and how they responded to that logic and we test whether the responses of institutions were those which policy-makers intended, i.e. did the policy achieve its intentions?

References

Allison, G. T. (1971) *Essence of Decision: Explaining the Cuban Missile Crisis*. Boston, Mass.: Little, Brown.

Barrett, S. and Fudge, C. (eds) (1981) *Policy and Action: Essays on the Implementation of Public Policy*. London: Methuen.

Davies, J. L. and Morgan, A. W. (1982) The Politics of Institutional Change. In Wagner, L. (ed.) *Agenda for Institutional Change in Higher Education*. Guildford: SRHE.

Dror, Y. (1968) *Public Policymaking Reexamined*. New York: Chandler.

Dror, Y. (1971) *Ventures in Policy Sciences*. London: Elsevier.

Dror, Y. (1986) *Policymaking under Adversity*. New Brunswick: Transaction.

Etzioni, A. (1967) Mixed Scanning: A Third Approach to Decision-Making. *Public Administration Review*, 27, pp. 385–92.

Hogwood, B. W. and Gunn, L. A. (1984) *Policy Analysis for the Real World*. Oxford: Oxford University Press.

Knight, P. (1981) The 1980–81 AFE Pool: the End of an Era. *Higher Education Review*, 14, No. 1, pp. 17–32.

Lindblom, C. E. (1959) The Science of 'Muddling through'. *Public Administration Quarterly*, XIX, pp. 79–88.

Locke, M. (undated) *Popper's Concept of Situational Logic: A grounding for theory in public administration*. CIS Working Paper No. 53. London: Centre for Institutional Studies, North East London Polytechnic.

Popper, K. (1960) *The Poverty of Historicism*. London: Routledge and Kegan Paul.

Popper, K. (1966) *The Open Society and its Enemies*. London: Routledge and Kegan Paul.

Popper, K. (1975) *Objective Knowledge*. Oxford: Oxford University Press.

Pratt, J. (1982) Resource Allocation Within the Public Sector. In Morris, A. and Sizer, J. (eds) *Resources and Higher Education*. Guildford: SRHE.

Pratt, J. (undated) *The Analysis and Testing of Public Policy*. CIS Working Paper No. 26. London: Centre for Institutional Studies, North East London Polytechnic.

Pressman, J. I. and Wildavsky, A. (1973) *Implementation*. Berkeley: University of California Press.

Quade, E. S. (1982) *Analysis for Public Decisions*. New York: Elsevier.

Shattock, M. and Rigby, G. (1983) *Resource Allocation in British Universities*. Guildford: SRHE.

Simon, H. A. (1947) *Administrative Behavior*. 1st edition. New York: Macmillan.

Simon, H. A. (1957a) *Administrative Behavior*. 2nd edition (with added introduction). New York: Macmillan.

Simon, H. A. (1957b) *Models of Man*. New York: John Wiley.

Simon, H. A. (1960) *The New Science of Management Decision*. Englewood Cliffs, NJ: Prentice Hall.

2

Public Sector Institutions
Facing Constraint

The public sector of higher education is the largest, fastest growing and most comprehensive part of the British higher education system. In 1984–5 there were over 300 institutions in this sector in England and Wales, and they contained 282 400 full-time and sandwich students and 199 200 part-time higher education students (DES 1986). Many public sector institutions also contained both full-time and part-time students on lower level courses; most of the students in higher education were concentrated in some 90 of the larger colleges. The university sector, by contrast, contains fewer than 50 institutions but slightly more full-time and sandwich students (290 600) than the public sector, though far fewer part-timers (36 000 plus 77 300 at the Open University). Total numbers in the public sector had grown by 25 per cent since 1979–80, universities' numbers by 2 per cent.

Perhaps the most obvious characteristic of the further education (FE) system is its variety – of types of colleges, courses, levels of work, methods of study and subject matter of courses. Courses offered cover practically every subject ever studied by man, and they can be followed by full-time, part-time, sandwich or block or day-release modes of study at different kinds of college – polytechnics, colleges of higher education, technical colleges, further education colleges, and so on. In any one college there are likely to be students studying at different levels, though most higher education or 'advanced' work is concentrated in the poly-technics and colleges of higher education, and it is distinguished by separate funding and administrative arrangements with which this study was concerned.

The principal characteristics of these arrangements derive from the fact that the institutions are part of the public education service. With some few exceptions they are run, in one way or another, by public authorities, mostly the local education authorities, as part of their statutory provision for further education, although the pattern is complicated by different arrangements in different parts of the country; in England and Wales the provision is made under the 1944 Education Act, though in England the Secretary of State for Education and Science is responsible for general policy direction, while in Wales it is the Secretary of State for Wales who has this responsibility. In Scotland (not considered further in this book) the responsibility lies with the Secretary of State for Scotland under different legislation.

The main exceptions to these arrangements are the group of voluntary colleges, financed directly by the Department of Education and Science, and three 'hybrid' colleges formed by mergers of voluntary and local authority colleges, which have voluntary status but which receive funding both from their local authorities and the DES.

2.1 The role of the local authorities

The prime duty in further education under the 1944 Education Act rests with the local authorities. Section 41 of the Act gives them the duty 'to secure the provision for their area of adequate facilities for further education. . .', though they do this under the general policy direction of the Secretary of State and the controls he exercises through legislation, regulation and other means, including financial. Thus, to secure the provision of 'adequate facilities', the local authorities operate under controls over building colleges, and the courses and curricula. In particular, in advanced further education, colleges wishing to put on courses have to get the approval of their governors, the local authority, the Regional Advisory Council (consisting of representatives of neighbouring LEAs, institutions and local industry) and the Secretary of State.

Institutional autonomy

Similarly, local authorities do not exercise day-to-day control over all aspects of their colleges. All major colleges have their own governing bodies and academic boards to give them a measure of independence and academic freedom. Governing bodies are appointed by the authority under the Education (No. 2) Act 1968 and usually consist of elected representatives of the authority, the college staff and students and nominees of relevant professional institutions, industry, etc. They have responsibility for the general direction of the college and varying measures of financial autonomy. The governors prepare and submit annual estimates to the authority and are generally free to spend within these estimates. Academic boards usually consist of the senior academic staff of the college, representatives of other staff and students. They are responsible for the overall academic policy of the college, subject to governors' and local authority policies. Within the general policy, the director or principal is responsible for day-to-day management and organization.

Finance

In the immediate post-war period, FE institutions served largely their local areas and LEA institutions were wholly financed by their maintaining authorities. Students from outside the local authority's area were paid for through 'recoupment' from their home authorities. As FE provision expanded recoupment became cumbersome, and a national 'pool' was created in 1958 for all advanced FE (AFE) provided by LEAs. LEAs contributed money to the pool theoretically in relation to the demand they made upon it, estimated from school population figures and non-domestic rateable values. Providing LEAs recouped funds according to their AFE provision estimated on the basis of teaching time devoted to advanced work. A separate pool operated for maintained teacher training institutions.

These arrangements operated unchanged in principle for 20 years, surviving even substantial institutional reforms such as the elimination of a separate teacher training sector and the subsequent amalgamation of the AFE and teacher training pools. It is important to note that there was no central government control of the pooling process except for technical work by the Pooling Committee. It was a mechanistic process with all spending decisions being taken at the LEA level, with the aggregate of spending forming the pool total.

The pool was widely criticized; its open-ended nature was said to allow providing LEAs to build up prestigious institutions at little or no cost to themselves; some (Lewis and Allemano 1972; Pratt 1976) criticized it as 'unfair' on both contributing and providing LEAs. Concern was expressed in the report of the Working Group on the Management of Public Sector Higher Education (the Oakes Report of 1978), that although the arrangements for controlling and financing higher education in the maintained sector

> have served well in a period of rapid growth they did not constitute an entirely satisfactory system of management and control and . . . their deficiences and the need for improved mechanisms for planning and controlling expenditure have become increasingly clear. (Oakes 1978)

In 1979 a major change transformed the pool overnight: it was decided to impose a cash limit upon the larger part of it from 1980–1. This 'capping' of the pool had major implications for the AFE sector. Decisions on spending taken in the past at LEA level now became effectively the subject of central control. Government sought a decision framework or yardstick with which to compare institutional spending. Initially, it decided to use a 'technical' method for allocating the funds and the allocations for the two financial years 1980–2 involved formulae largely based on past expenditure levels which were widely regarded as unsatisfactory (Knight 1981; CIS 1980). In 1982–3 a unit cost method was used and the principles of this method have formed the basis for resource allocation since then.

2.2 The National Advisory Body

At the same time, government was seeking institutional as well as financial changes. In 1981 discussion was initiated on long-term arrangements for a 'central focus' to 'oversee the financing and management of higher education outside the universities' (DES 1981). As an 'interim' measure, arrangements were made to establish the National Advisory Body for Local Authority Higher

Education which started work at the beginning of 1982. In its initial, interim form NAB's remit covered only institutions maintained by local education authorities; later this was widened to include voluntary colleges. Its title was also altered to the National Advisory Body for Public Sector Higher Education to reflect its wider role. From then on, the AFE Pool was allocated on the advice of NAB.

The National Advisory Body has a three-tier structure reflecting the complexities of the public sector system. The top tier is a Committee chaired by the junior Minister responsible for higher education and consisting of eight elected members of local authorities appointed by the local authority associations. It takes the final decisions on the advice of the Minister. The main debates take place in the Board, whose chairman is appointed by the Secretary of State, and which consists of about 20 members nominated by the various interests in the sector including institutions, teacher unions, local authorities, etc. The third tier is a range of sub-committees and subject boards with other members from the system and outside it, reporting to the Board, whose advice in turn is reported to the Committee. There is also a relatively small professional secretariat.

Formally, NAB is responsible for advising the Secretary of State on two principal areas: the apportionment of resources from the Advanced Further Education pool, and the academic provision to be made by each institution. Additional areas of responsibility include offering advice on allocation of resources for capital spending, the approval of advanced courses, coordination of provision both within the public sector and between the public and university sectors, and monitoring of the implementation of policy decisions taken by the Secretary of State in the light of the advice offered.

NAB assumed responsibility for advising on the distribution of the AFE pool for 1983–4. The method initially adopted represented a continuation of an historic unit funding approach first introduced the previous year, albeit with a number of refinements. It was in respect of 1984–5 that NAB conducted its first major planning exercise. This exercise was without question a watershed in English public sector higher education. It marked a fundamental change to a system of centralized planning and overall control of PSHE and raised important questions concerning the equitability of treatment of individual institutions.

Financial constraint

The first problem that NAB faced was that of financial constraint. The annual expenditure targets for higher education had been progressively constrained. The process began in the early 1970s, though few noticed its significance at the time, with the 1972 White Paper *Education: A Framework for Expansion*. A year later, the 1973 expenditure White Paper proposed reductions in recurrent and capital spending. By 1976 there were severe restrictions on capital spending and, after the election of a Conservative government in 1979, further constraint meant that the 1981 expenditure White Paper presaged cuts, according to one commentator, of 10 000 staff representing one in six teaching posts in higher education together with a loss of some 30 000 student places and a drop in the age participation rate (Ashworth 1983). By the time NAB began its 1983–4 planning exercise, the real value of the AFE Pool was expected to diminish by about 10 per cent to £560.5 m over the 2 years to 1984–5. How to distribute this diminished sum to a complex system of colleges was what might be termed the immediate problem facing the NAB in its planning exercise. There was, however, more to the problem, as the details of the planning exercise, which we consider in Chapter 3, reveal.

References

Ashworth, J. (1983) Reshaping Higher Education in Britain. *Higher Education Review*, Spring 1983.

Centre for Institutional Studies (1980) The Funding and Control of Advanced Further Education. *Commentary*, No. 11. North East London Polytechnic.

Department of Education and Science (1981) *Higher Education in England Outside the Universities: Policy, Funding and Management, A Consultative Document*, July 1981, mimeo.

Department of Education and Science (1986) *Student Numbers in Higher Education – Great Britain 1979 to 1984.* Statistical Bulletin 14/86.

Knight, P. (1981) The 1980–81 AFE Pool: The End of an Era. *Higher Education Review*, 14, No. 1, pp. 17–32.

Lewis, P. and Allemano, R. (1972) Fact and Fiction about the Pool. *Higher Education Review*, Spring 1972.

Oakes, G. (Chairman) (1978) *Report of the Working Group on the Management of Higher Education in the Maintained Sector.* Cmnd. 7130. London: HMSO.

Pratt, J. (1976) Pooling, Some Revised Conclusions. *Higher Education Review*, Spring 1976.

3

The NAB Planning Exercise

In order to understand how government policy was implemented through the first NAB exercise, we need to examine some of the details of NAB's deliberations and the bases on which its decisions were made. In this chapter, we present a timetable of the exercise, followed by an examination of the process of decision-making, first on the distribution of student numbers and then on the funding methodology. Finally, we examine the outcomes of the exercise for the institutions and NAB's role in the policy-making process.

3.1 Timetable

A marked feature of the NAB planning exercise was the speed with which it was conducted: somewhat less than 18 months elapsed between the notification to the institutions of the decision to hold the exercise and its formal completion; the exercise proper lasted just over 14 months. The timetable of the exercise was, in outline, as follows.

26 July 1982

An initial letter outlining the timing and proposed stages of the planning exercise was sent to the institutions. This informed institutions that total expenditure on public sector higher education was anticipated to fall by 10 per cent in real terms between 1982–3 and 1984–5 and that course provision would need to be planned on this basis. Institutions would be required to submit plans on different hypothetical levels of expenditure for 1984–5 compared with 1982–3 while paying regard to the need to balance considerations of access and the unit of resource, balance of entry by level and mode of study, and the speed with which shifts in provision could be affected. A first indication was also given of the special status to be accorded to sub-degree level and part-time provision and to the likelihood of a request to prioritize particular areas of provision when plans were drawn up.

30 September 1982

This letter set in train the exercise proper by inviting institutions to draw up plans for their AFE work in 1984–5 in 14 programme areas assuming a 10 per cent reduction in real terms expenditure between 1982–3 and 1984–5. The plans which were to contain a similar statement of actual work in 1982–3 and a revenue statement for that year, were to be submitted to NAB via the LEA. The letter asked institutions to provide details of student load by programme and to specify those programme areas regarded as having the highest priority. Institutional planning was to be completed by the end of December for consideration and possible amendment by the LEA during the spring.

The programme areas within which plans were to be presented had been developed by the NAB from DES list 209 of subject classifications used for the Further Education Statistical Record (FESR) with the addition of teacher training. A list of the 14 programmes areas can be found in Table 3.1.

The letter emphasized the need to consider the academic quality of courses, the balance between maintaining student numbers at lower unit costs and reducing intakes, and the special status which was to be attached to sub-degree level and part-time provision. It also pointed out that the assumption of a 10 per cent real terms reduction in expenditure referred to the sum of pool and home (plus EEC) students' fees and not a 10 per cent reduction in pool income to which the appropriate fee income could later be added. A further letter was despatched on the same date to the LEAs. After explaining what was being asked of the institutions this letter asked LEAs to amend institutions' plans where appropriate and to submit to NAB a separate planning return for each polytechnic and major college and an aggregated return for all other AFE providers which they maintained. LEAs were also asked to inform the institutions what 'topping-up' funding, if any, was likely to be made available in 1984–5, so that this information could be incorporated into the planning process.

26 August 1983: the 'indicative allocation'

Having completed the initial stages of its planning, NAB notified the institutions of proposed student target totals by programme for 1984–5, expressed as student full-time equivalents (FTEs). This letter also provided what was termed an 'indicative net pool allocation figure' for 1984–5 which had been derived from the target student enrolments. It was emphasized that all of the figures provided were to be regarded as tentative and, while the target enrolments reflected planned overall provision, no final decision on the funding methodology had been taken. Written comments were invited to reach NAB not later than 19 September. Similar notification was sent to the LEAs.

The proposed targets reflected advice given to NAB by the Secretary of State in a letter of 21 February 1983 on the pool 'quantum' and on the priority that he hoped would be given to scientific and technological provision of value to industry. The major problem faced by NAB had been the need to reconcile the conflicting criteria of maintaining and improving access to public sector higher education with the safeguarding of educational standards by maintaining, as far as possible, the unit of resource. At an early stage of the exercise it was accepted by NAB that access was to be the overriding consideration and that revenue expenditure per student would therefore have to fall. Nevertheless, unease concerning this trade-off continued and, following a meeting with the Secretary of State, it was announced in October 1983 that an additional £20 m would be made available to supplement the previously planned pool quantum. This produced a total of £580. 5 m for distribution to the institutions.

9 December 1983

NAB published its advice to the Secretary of State (NAB 1983a), and notified the institutions of:

1. Target student enrolments for 1984–5 by programme.
2. Implied first year student numbers by programme, derived from 1982–3 actual enrolments and 1984–5 targets.
3. Maxima for the institution as a whole for (i) the number of students on first and higher degree courses and (ii) the number of full-time and sandwich students.
4. The allocation of funding from the capped AFE pool as recommended to the Secretary of State.

Its advice acknowledged the difficulties inherent in the move to externally determined enrolments by stressing that all of the figures were to be regarded as targets rather than fixed limits. Nevertheless, the establishment of maxima for first and higher degree work and for full-time and sandwich students was considered essential in order to protect provision for sub-degree level and part-time students. Institutions were nevertheless advised that the implied part-time and sub-degree level enrolment figures should also be regarded as targets rather than fixed limits, but it was pointed out that NAB expected any deviation from targets to favour sub-degree level and part-time provision rather than higher level work.

3.2 The distribution of student numbers

In its advice to the Secretary of State, NAB discussed the considerations which had informed its planning as well as some of the likely consequences. The criteria involved in arriving at the distribution of target student numbers were:

1. A wish to maintain and enhance access to public sector higher education.
2. The need to establish a minimum unit of resource to protect standards.

3. A wish to protect provision of part-time and sub-degree level work.
4. A wish to give favourable treatment to particular areas of provision in line with the guidance given by the Secretary of State.
5. The need to provide a balanced geographical distribution of provision, particularly in relation to part-time work, and to arrest the recent concentration of provision in London and the Home Counties.

All these criteria had to be considered in the context of an exercise requiring the participation of the institutions themselves. NAB asked the institutions to respond with their own plans for future enrolments and NAB officials made it clear that they expected to take these 'bids' into consideration. NAB rejected the concept of 'equal misery' and expected institutions to evaluate their academic profiles and decide their own priorities in order to maintain the best quality courses. They asked institutions to search their academic work in terms of higher or lower priority for each programme area.

The division of all courses into 14 programme areas itself created considerable problems for institutions, especially those with modular or interdisciplinary courses. There were negotiations between NAB and the institutions on the correct classification of various courses. Because the overall level and distribution of funding was not decided at the time of the preliminary allocation of student numbers (August 1983), there were considerable changes for many institutions between their preliminary and final student number targets.

The advice given to the Secretary of State thus reflected decisions on the size, composition and deployment of the planned student population. The aggregated institutional plans were based on a target enrolment across the country of 260 314 FTEs, an increase of 7.5 per cent on the 1982–3 actual enrolments. Within this, the planned total number of full-time and sandwich students – 197 081 FTEs – was 8 per cent higher than in 1982–3, while that of part-time students – 63 233 FTEs – was 6 per cent higher. At sub-degree level, planned enrolments were 9.9 per cent higher than 1982–3 (100 200 FTEs), while first degree and higher level enrolments were planned to rise by 6.1 per cent to 160 000 FTEs. Increases in target enrolment figures ranged between 10 per cent in the North and East Anglia and 4 per cent in the East Midlands. The distribution of target enrolments by programmes was the area where the most marked changes were found. Table 3.1 shows the proposed changes.

Overall student numbers were planned to grow most in programmes H (Mathematics and Computer Studies), F (Agriculture, Forestry and Veterinary Studies), and E and N (Other Technology and Manufacture, and Music, Drama and Visual Arts, respectively). Only one programme, M (Humanities), was planned to shrink absolutely, and that by 2 per cent. However, the distribution of first year enrolments (full-time and sandwich students only) was planned to change much more severely. Programme H was planned to expand by 47 per cent, programme D (Engineering) by 15 per cent and programme F by 13 per cent. At the other end of the scale first year enrolments in programme J (Social and Administrative Studies) were planned to fall by 9 per cent, and in programme M by 18 per cent.

Table 3.1   *Actual Enrolments 1982–3 and Target Enrolments 1984–5*

Programme[a]	All years			First year only[b]		
	Actual (1982–3)	Target (1984–5)	% change	Actual (1982–3)	Target (1984–5)	% change
A	17 048	17 887	4.92	8 368	8 038	−3.58
B	6 798	7 150	5.17	1 406	1 363	−3.05
C	9 330	9 984	7.00	3 505	3 474	−0.88
D	42 480	46 630	9.76	10 238	11 772	14.98
E	6 411	7 091	10.60	2 058	2 258	9.71
F	698	852	22.06	252	285	13.09
G	18 694	20 484	9.57	6 721	7 163	6.57
H	9 667	12 304	27.27	3 672	5 398	47.00
I	51 588	54 899	6.41	15 975	16 678	4.40
J	22 271	22 640	1.65	8 864	8 063	−9.03
K	13 756	17 657	5.37	6 974	6 984	0.14
L	6 548	6 713	2.51	2 279	2 157	−5.35
M	11 886	11 689	−1.65	4 829	3 952	−18.16
N	21 966	24 334	10.78	9 296	8 905	−4.20
Total	242 141	260 314	7.50	84 437	86 520	2.46

[a]Key to programme areas: A Initial teacher training; B In-service teacher training and other education; C Medicine, dentistry, pharmacy and ancillary health subjects; D Engineering; E Other technology and manufacture; F Agriculture, forestry and veterinary studies; G Science, applied science; H Mathematics and computer studies; I Business management, accountancy and law; J Social and administrative studies; K Other professional and vocational studies; L Languages and literature; M Humanities; N Music, drama and visual arts.
[b] All figures for first year enrolments relate to full-time and sandwich students only.
Source: NAB (1983a).

3.3 The 1984–5 funding methodology

Deciding the pattern of provision in terms of target student numbers was one thing, and complicated enough. Allocating resources from the AFE Pool to institutions to support this – and to conform to further criteria – was as confusing as the planning exercise. NAB's decisions on the distribution of the AFE pool in 1984–5 were marked by a good deal of ambiguity and confusion. During the course of its deliberations NAB examined and discarded three distinct methodologies for determining allocations from the AFE pool. At each stage institutions watched anxiously trying to predict the consequences for each of them, often reacting with alarm or despair.

Essentially, the purpose of this part of the planning exercise was to produce a funding distribution which:

1. Penalized high-cost institutions by cutting the average unit of resource.
2. Rewarded those institutions regarded as efficient by maintaining and, in some instances, increasing the funding to be made available.
3. Related funding to the planned target number and mix of students.

4. Supported as far as possible the academic criteria on which the decisions on student enrolments were based.

The initial basis of the allocation given to each institution was its target student enrolment. These target enrolments were derived from the aggregate enrolment of 260 314 which had been determined by NAB. In order to arrive at institutional target enrolments the figures provided by the institutions' own planning returns were taken as the starting point. These were aggregated for local authority higher education as a whole and then distributed first between the 72 subject divisions used for the FESR returns and later consolidated into the 14 programme areas developed by NAB (see Table 3.1). This final distribution was made, as far as possible, to reflect the advice given by the Secretary of State on 21 February 1983 on priority subject areas while recognizing the need to avoid disruption or damaging shifts in non-preferred areas. Net programme weights derived from a planning exercise conducted by HMI were then applied to the institutions' targets to produce programme-weighted target enrolment figures for each institution.

The HMI planning exercise

The incorporation of these programme weights based on the HMI exercise was a crucial stage of the funding methodology and has had important implications for institutions. The data on which the weightings were based have been widely perceived as targets or guidelines to be followed within institutions. We therefore set out the basis of this exercise as briefly as possible, though necessarily presenting some detail.

The planning exercise undertaken by HMI was designed to produce 'best practice' data for teaching and non-teaching costs in each of the FESR subject areas. This exercise proceeded on the basis of HMI's 'knowledge of the system' gained during the normal course of work, supplemented by visits by subject specialists to a spectrum of institutions. It was emphasized, when the results of this exercise were presented to NAB, that

> the figures represent[ed] HMI's view, based on observation of good practice of 'what ought to be' rather than 'what is' and that they are based on relatively large units of provision with balanced full-time and part-time populations where economies of scale are possible. (NAB 1983b)

Initially, four figures were produced in respect of each subject area. The first of these, the best-practice student:staff ratio (SSR), was designed to permit calculations of notional teaching costs. These best-practice SSRs are shown in Table 3.2. The remaining three figures were referred to as normalized cost factors (NCFs) and related to notional non-teaching costs:

1. Educational support staff (technicians, etc.).
2. Recurrent expenditure on books, equipment and materials (excluding major capital items).

Table 3.2   *Best-practice SSRs*

Programme		SSR
A	Teacher Training	12
B	INSET	12
C	Medicine and Health	10
D	Engineering	11.87
E	Other Technology	11.56
F	Agriculture	15
G	Science	10.21
H	Maths and Computing	10.8
I	Business, etc.	13.73
J	Social Science	12.43
K	Other Professional	10.53
L	Languages	13.05
M	Humanities	15
N	Music, Drama, Art	9
Average		11.88

Source: NAB (1984).

3. Recurrent premises costs directly associated with the teaching of a subject (heating, lighting, maintenance, etc.).

All of the figures produced were designed to represent cost relativities rather than the actual cost of teaching a subject. The information produced by HMI was passed to DES accountants for conversion to cost relativities for subjects and NAB programmes. In order to make these conversions two assumptions were necessary, namely: (i) the distribution of students by subject, and (ii) the distribution of total expenditure between the four categories under which HMI had provided data.

In deciding on these distributions the only consistent available source of information on the distribution of students was the 1981 FESR. The student distribution which this showed, when combined with the HMI data on SSRs, implied a SSR for public sector higher education as a whole of 11.7. This figure in turn when applied to average Burnham salary data implied that 51 per cent of the anticipated pool quantum for 1984–5 should be devoted to teaching costs. This represented a drop of 3 per cent on the 1981–2 figure. The remaining 49 per cent was then split between non-teaching costs so as to maintain the proportions of out-turn expenditure found in 1981–2. Of the three elements of non-teaching costs (listed above) for which HMI had supplied data, the proportions of the quantum assigned to each were 6.8 per cent, 7.6 per cent and 13.4 per cent, respectively. The remaining 21.2 per cent was then divided equally among all FTE students and was presumed to cover one-third of support staff, one-quarter of premises costs and all administrative and miscellaneous costs.

These data were then converted to relative subject weights by multiplying the number of FTE students in each area by the appropriate NCF to produce an overall number of cost units for each subject. These non-teaching cost figures were then applied to the percentage figures given above in order to derive relative non-teaching costs. When combined with relative teaching cost data aggregated subject weightings were produced.

A broadly similar approach was adopted to convert subject weightings to programme weightings. Once again, 1981 FESR data were used as the basis for assumptions on the subject distribution of students within programmes. All figures were produced initially on a gross basis and subsequently on a net basis by deduction of assumed fee income. The cheapest programme was found to be Humanities (M) which was given a weight of 1.0 and the other programmes were then scaled relative to this.

The DES emphasized that the details of weightings were dependent on the division of student numbers by subject, and the percentages of expenditure allotted to each of the five elements. Thus if either of these were altered then the subject and programme weights, which were designed to reflect cost relativities assuming best-practice operation, would change also.

Institutional pool allocations

The procedure for calculating institutional pool allocations was also complicated and involved a number of stages. The total size of the quantum was £580.5 m following the £20 m supplementation which had been agreed by the Secretary of State. From this, £300 000 was deducted to support a number of specific new initiatives in Information Technology, the remainder being split into four 'sub-quanta' for allocation to four groups of institutions: the polytechnics, major institutions (defined by reference to size and proportion of work at advanced level), four monotechnics, and all other AFE providers.

Allocations to the four monotechnics (Rose Bruford College of Speech and Drama, Camborne School of Mines, Kent College for the Careers Service and Royal Northern College of Music) were calculated first by subtracting 5 per cent from their 1982–3 out-turn expenditure. The remaining £576.8 m was then split between the three remaining categories of institutions so as to broadly maintain the proportion of the pool received by each category in 1983–4. Table 3.3 shows the distribution of the pool between each sub-sector in 1983–4 and 1984–5.

After account had been taken of London Weighting this distribution of funds provided an initial net unit of resource for each sub-sector when target enrolments were applied to the relevant sub-quanta. These figures were polytechnics (£1477), major OMEs (£1257) and minor OMEs (£1179). Allocations were then derived. The target enrolment based on programme weightings (and where appropriate enhanced by a London Weighting factor) was multiplied by the net unit of resource for the category of institution. Per capita sums were then added in respect of catering and residence in order to produce basic allocations. This allocation was then 'moderated' 50 per cent year on year against the 1983–4 allocation adjusted to the 1984–5 base: where the unmoderated figure was greater than the adjusted 1983–4 allocation then the increase

Table 3.3 *Distribution of Pool to Sub-sectors,*
£m (percentage share in brackets)

Sub-sector	1983–4	1984–5
Polytechnics	377.7 (67.6)	388.6 (67.4)
Major OMEs	79.7 (14.3)	83.8 (14.5)
Minor OMEs	101.0 (18.1)	104.4 (18.1)
Total	558.4	576.8

Source: NAB (1983a, p. 19).

was halved; where it was less the loss was halved. However, it had also been decided that no institution should be subject to a cut in allocation greater than 5 per cent in cash terms. When these institutions' allocations were made up to this level, the allocations of all other institutions were scaled down to ensure that the total remained within the pool quantum.

Finally, a minimum net unit of resource of £1250 per FTE for Humanities (the base programme) was set for polytechnics and major colleges because the previous stages of the process had the effect of shifting resources towards the

Table 3.4 *Programme Weighting Factors and Implied Minimum Net Unit of Resource for Polytechnics and Major OMEs*

	Programme	Weighting factors	Implies Net minimum unit of resource (£)
A	Initial Teacher Training	1.4	1750
B	In-service Teacher Training and other education	1.5	1875
C	Medicine, Dentistry, Pharmacy and ancillary health subjects	1.9	2375
D	Engineering	1.8	2250
E	Other Technology and Manufacture	1.6	2000
F	Agriculture, Forestry and Veterinary Studies	1.4	1750
G	Science, Applied Science	1.9	2375
H	Mathematics and Computer Studies	2.1	2625
I	Business Management, Accountancy and Law	1.2	1500
J	Social and Administrative Studies	1.3	1625
K	Other Professional and Vocational Studies	1.6	2000
L	Language and Literature	1.2	1500
M	Humanities	1.0	1250
N	Music, Drama and Visual Arts	1.9	2375

Source: NAB (1983a). Implied net minimum unit of resource by calculation (weighting factors times £1250)

more expensive institutions, and in some instances moderated allocations had fallen below this minimum. Allocations for these institutions were increased and those to all other major providers scaled down again to contain the total within the Pool quantum. Table 3.4 shows the effect of the introduction of this floor-funding level for polytechnics and major colleges. It is emphasized that the actual units of resource for all polytechnics and many major colleges were higher than those shown in the table, as those institutions receiving above the minimum were not affected by this stage of the allocation.

3.4 The outcome for institutions

The overall effect of the NAB funding methodology was that allocations to institutions were determined by the sub-sector in which they were located, their NAB target student enrolments and programme mix and their historic pattern of expenditure and enrolments. No two institutions were entirely alike in the impact of these factors and hence considerable variations were found both in 1984–5 allocations and in year on year changes. Furthermore, because different methodologies were used, there were also considerable variations between institutions in their indicative and final allocations. Table 3.5 shows these changes. Two points need to be made. First, while the aggregate target enrolment expanded by nearly 6000 FTEs between August and December 1983, institutional targets were changed considerably by NAB, so that changes in Pool distribution would have occurred even if the allocation methodology had not. Secondly, the final allocations were based on the enhanced quantum produced by the £20 m supplementation agreed by the Secretary of State in October 1983. Hence some increases in allocations arise from this. Nevertheless, these changes added a further element of unpredictability to an already complicated system, and compounded the difficulties of planning for institutions.

3.5 NAB's policy-making role

When we examine the first NAB planning exercise, we find that the implementation of government policy was not a linear process of putting policy into practice. In fact, the NAB exercise was itself part of the policy-making process: NAB was expected to work out a methodology for the distribution of funding and student numbers between institutions, as well as advising the Secretary of State on the overall size of the pool allocation for 1984–5. This amount and its distribution were not finalized until the very end of the NAB exercise in December 1983. In the course of the exercise, NAB experimented with several different funding methodologies and the Secretary of State indicated that he would like certain subject areas to be given higher priorities. All these decisions were taken after institutions had responded to the original premise of a 10 per cent reduction in resources. The rules of the game changed in the course of the exercise, but the institutions' responses were still regarded as 'bids' by NAB, and these bids played an important part in NAB's decision on how to allocate student numbers and funding to individual institutions.

The complexities of the timing were compounded by the many and sometimes contradictory goals of the NAB exercise. NAB was responsible for advising on the distribution of both funding and student numbers to individual institutions. Many criteria were taken into consideration in the determination of these distributions. The government was concerned to reduce expenditure on

Table. 3.5   *AFE Pool Allocations 1983–4 and 1984–5 Plus Indicative Allocation for 1984–5*

Polytechnics	A NAB actual allocations 1983–4	B 1984–5	C % change Col. A–B	D NAB indicative allocation	% change col. A–D
NELP	16.485	15.599	−5.37	13.875	−15.83
Middlesex	15.933	15.992	0.37	14.650	−8.05
Kingston	12.344	13.232	7.19	12.231	−0.91
Birmingham	12.576	13.098	4.15	12.506	−0.55
Coventry	13.721	13.799	0.56	13.106	−4.48
Wolverhampton	12.203	12.444	1.95	11.864	−2.79
Liverpool	17.489	17.831	16.26	14.910	−2.78
Manchester	21.908	23.191	2.30	22.334	−1.47
Sheffield	18.805	19.372	3.01	18.436	−1.96
Huddersfield	10.572	10.847	2.54	10.227	−3.26
Leeds	14.005	14.709	5.02	13.882	−0.87
Newcastle	15.051	15.820	5.10	14.928	−0.81
Sunderland	9.717	10.009	3.00	9.704	−0.13
North London	10.917	11.223	2.80	10.429	−4.47
South Bank	14.178	14.261	0.58	12.974	−8.49
City	8.505	8.752	−1.72	7.652	−14.08
Central London	11.577	11.171	−3.50	10.185	−12.02
Thames	8.906	9.032	1.39	8.352	−6.24
Bristol	13.299	13.939	4.81	13.402	0.77
Teesside	7.280	8.081	11.00	7.700	5.76
Plymouth	9.152	10.355	13.14	9.855	7.68
Brighton	12.683	12.868	1.45	12.337	−2.72
Portsmouth	15.660	15.550	−0.70	13.901	−11.23
Hatfield	11.749	11.866	14.00	9.933	−4.56
Preston	9.486	10.291	8.48	9.759	2.87
Leicester	15.253	16.104	5.57	15.551	1.95
Trent	17.985	18.219	1.30	17.414	−3.17
Oxford	9.541	9.882	3.57	9.136	−4.24
North Staffs	10.577	11.319	7.01	10.912	3.16
Total	375.229	388.850	3.63	362.145	−3.48

Source: THES 16 December 1983.

higher education, but it was reluctant to see access to the public sector reduced. NAB was expected to develop a funding methodology which would reward the more 'efficient' institutions, but at the same time it had to find a politically acceptable distribution, taking into account the strong local authority representation on the NAB board. NAB experimented with various highly mechanistic approaches which gave the appearance of objectivity, but the result could not vary too much from previous years or it would mean wholesale closures of courses or institutions.

The distribution of student numbers also involved opposing objectives. NAB wished to protect the provision of part-time and sub-degree level work, but DES standard indicators of 'efficiency' (such as staff–student ratios) on which the resources for various levels of work were based, tended to favour full-time degree courses. NAB had to respond to the Secretary of State's desire to give favourable treatment to particular areas of provision, but it was also expected to consider a balanced geographical distribution and the need to establish a minimum unit of resource to protect standards.

Considering all these opposing priorities it is not surprising that NAB sent conflicting signals to institutions or that the rules of the game changed in the course of the exercise. What the allocation methodology achieved was a funding distribution which bore a sufficiently close relationship to 1983–4 allocations to prove acceptable to NAB and the Secretary of State. In November 1983 advice was offered to the NAB Board from one of its working groups that

> the final choice of the advice to be offered to the Secretary of State [should] rest on judgements about the outcome of the preferred methodology, rather than on strong convictions about the preferred methodological principles. (NAB 1983c)

Expediency was the major factor in determining not only the pool distribution methodology but also the level at which resources should be allocated to individual institutions. Indeed, if the underlying rationale of the sub-quantum approach was to reduce income to those institutions regarded as expensive while rewarding the more efficient, then a similar effect could have been achieved much more simply by rolling forward 1983–4 allocations adjusted on a judgemental basis to the mean unit of resource. Such an approach would have been very similar in principle to the funding mechanism proposed by the DES but abandoned by NAB and could, depending on the schedule of change adopted, have produced a similar distribution to the sub-quantum without much of the technical complexity of that approach.

Hence, while the highly mechanistic approach represented by the sub-quantum methodology may give the appearance of objectivity, the existence of such factors as the 5 per cent maximum reduction, the 50 per cent moderation and the £1250 minimum unit of resource point toward a high level of subjectivity. The complexity of the methodology, the changes it underwent and the time-scale of the planning exercise were widely seen by institutions as making planning and the management of constraint more difficult.

References

National Advisory Body (1983a) Advice from NAB on 1984–85 Allocations to Sir Keith Joseph, 9 December 1983.

National Advisory Body (1983b) Technical and Data Group Paper 19/83.

National Advisory Body (1983c) NAB Board Paper 107/83, para. 4.

National Advisory Body (1984) Technical and Data Group Paper 36/84 Times Higher Education Supplement, 16 December 1983.

4

The Study

The brief agreed with the Department of Education and Science proposed a research programme with two main components: a short contextual study of the circumstances of PSHE at the time of the NAB planning exercise and a series of case studies of institutions. From the case studies would be developed a final report identifying the main findings of the study. The brief identified a number of areas of investigation or 'themes' which were refined and further developed in Steering Group discussions. As we noted in Chapter 1, each of the research teams took responsibility for a number of these themes, so this chapter, like the rest of the book, is based mainly on the methodology developed by the team from the Centre for Institutional Studies.

1 Aims

The project brief identified a number of aims for this study. It was, first, descriptive. It was to identify and record how institutions perceived and responded to the constraints placed upon them by financial reductions in general, and the NAB exercise in particular.

The second aim of the study was to be analytical and, it was hoped, prescriptive, and it was here that the study turned to the main questions with which this book is concerned. Our analysis can be seen as a test of two sets of actions. The first of these was the study's main focus, the management responses of the institutions to constraint. Thus we sought to identify the policy choices that were perceived by managers and others in the institutions and the ways that they responded to them. We tried to identify the processes used to determine their responses, and to deal with their consequences in so far as they became known during the study. We were trying to establish how far the responses conformed with such advice on 'good management' as is available from management literature, and whether there were lessons of good and bad practice from the experience of the institutions studied that could be of benefit to other institutions. As a by-product, the advice of the literature could be considered as having undergone a brisk test under fire in the institutions.

The second set of actions that were under test in this study were those of the actors and agencies setting the framework within which institutions had to operate. In other words, the study necessarily involved a test of the efficacy and appropriateness of the process of NAB itself. Was this a good framework within which institutions could make decisions?

The third aim of the study was to identify, so far as possible, the factors affecting the responses of the institutions. How far did the responses derive from or were conditioned by the history, circumstances or internal structures and processes of the institution? At the same time, we sought to see whether some of these factors were affected in turn by constraint and the NAB exercise. Did institutions change their structures, or processes of management and control, in response to new circumstances? Here, too, we hoped to find out about which factors were helpful and which not, and which processes or structures institutions might look to in times of constraint.

4.2   Methodological issues

A study such as this, commissioned to monitor and evaluate a major and controversial national planning exercise, raises a number of methodological issues as well as facing practical problems. The methodological issues were mainly ones of approach, and the selection of institutions and techniques. The practical problems mostly arose from the timing and time-scale of the project, which in turn had methodological implications. Both were compounded by the fact that there were two research teams 200 miles apart.

There are, of course, the many basic problems common to studies in the social sciences in general and of organizations in particular, which we need not discuss in detail here. We recognize, for example, that no 'description' is without theoretical assumptions and implications; that 'observations' are not theory-free; that there are substantial problems of establishing an accurate record of what took place and the relationship, if any, between events. Suffice it to say that since we subscribe to a Popperian epistemology, we seek to test hypotheses intersubjectively against observable events, recognizing that the descriptions of these events are themselves, as we noted above, theory-bound. So when we speak, as we do above, of our first aim being to describe the institutions' responses to the NAB exercise, this description is set in the context of the policy and management literature which we refer to in our second aim. Similarly, although we see ourselves as observers and analysers of what took place, with all the hazards and problems that this raises, we would not term this a 'positivist' approach of the kind identified in sometimes oversimplified descriptions of research method (e.g. Cohen and Manion 1985) nor as an entirely 'illuminative' or 'interpretive' approach, though within our framework we employ illuminative techniques to generate evidence. Our concern was to see the study as a test of the management responses of the institutions and of the policy and administrative framework within which these responses were made.

The idea of testing the management responses of the institutions does of course imply that consequences follow from – or more accurately are held to follow from – the decisions and actions of institutional managers. We do not, however, reject the possibility (or perhaps probability) that other factors may be at work and that formal structures, processes and decisions are not the only determinants of events.

Time-scale and timing

At the practical level, the time-scale of the project was strictly limited. It was commissioned in September 1983 for 2 years with the delivery of the final report scheduled for December 1985. This deadline was insisted on by the DES who wished for a report and any lessons learned to be available as soon after the completion of the NAB exercise as possible, and we are pleased to report it was maintained by the project team.

This timetable sharply limited the scope of fieldwork in the institutions. Although 2 years seems a long time, allowance has to be made for gaining access to institutions, establishing methodologies and working relationships, and later for analysing data and case and report writing. The institutions, too, were geographically far-flung. In the event, most institutional visits began early in 1984 and finished by Easter 1985. All the case studies and the final report were written within the short period of time from then until the end of the year.

The time-scale of the project compounded the problems of its timing. The NAB exercise began before the research was commissioned, so that we faced the problem of trying to reconstruct events, as well as record them as they happened, but many of the consequences of the exercise in terms of student enrolment and curricular changes would not be visible for the most part until after September 1985 (and even then some data would not be assembled until 1986), after the project had finished. The research team and the Steering Group were unable to persuade the DES that an extension would enable data of value to be collected. All this means that our conclusions are in places more tentative than they might have been. It is difficult to be assertive about 'good management' when the outcomes of the actions are not yet fully known.

Selection of case study institutions

A further practical problem arose from the size of public sector higher education. The sector consists of several hundred colleges of disparate character, ranging from polytechnics with national or international standing to small colleges with perhaps one or two advanced courses. It was recognized from the start of the project that if management responses were to be studied in any detail at all, a sample of colleges would need to be selected.

The selection of the sample presented substantive problems. It was clear that neither comprehensive coverage, nor even a truly representative group of the bewildering variety of public sector institutions, could be studied. Selecting a representative sample is almost impossible because of the difficulty of identifying, let alone agreeing, the defining characteristics and the probability that there could be as many of these as institutions. Instead, a case study approach was adopted. The institutions were selected for particular characteristics, though we attempted to maintain some broad representation of the major kinds of colleges and the treatment they received during the NAB exercise.

The eight institutions finally selected were generally among the largest in the sector, on the grounds that the DES was most concerned with the management problems of these kinds of institutions. Some institutions were selected on the size of the cut they received under the NAB exercise; we chose one polytechnic with severe cuts, and another receiving additional funds. Other institutions were included because they were known to have responded in particular ways to the NAB exercise. The research team had originally proposed a sample of six institutions be used, four polytechnics and two colleges of higher education. The DES suggested five polytechnics and one college. After negotiations with institutions, four polytechnics and two colleges agreed to be involved in the project. Then, the Steering Group advised that two more colleges of higher education be added, particularly one of a smaller size. So the final selection contained four polytechnics and four colleges, two of the latter 'hybrid' colleges with voluntary status. The four institutions geographically most conveniently located were allocated to each research team for data collection and the writing of case studies. Comparability was assisted by a common format agreed for the cases by the Steering Committee; researchers from each team also made visits to the other's institutions.

4.3   The case study institutions

The institutions were geographically widely spread, with the polytechnics in Yorkshire, Greater London, the South-west and the Midlands, and colleges in London and the Midlands and on the south and east coasts. They ranged in size from over 7000 FTE students in the largest polytechnic to 4300 in the smallest; three of the colleges had over 2000 students, one had about 900. Several of the institutions specialized in particular subject areas, two polytechnics concentrating on applied sciences and engineering, while one of the colleges offered mainly teacher education and humanities courses and another had developed in business and management studies, languages and professional and vocational courses. Several of the institutions, too, had been involved in mergers with colleges of education and one of these was still in the process of completing such a merger during the planning exercise. The individual institutions can be briefly described as follows:

Polytechnic A

A large urban polytechnic, with about 5800 FTE students at the time of the planning exercise. Formed from the merger of three colleges in 1970 it was located on a variety of sites. Its five faculties at the time of the exercise covered science, engineering, management, arts and social sciences.

Polytechnic B

This was the largest institution in our sample with over 7000 students and an emphasis on science and engineering. It was formed in 1969 from a college of technology and a college of art, and merged in 1976 with two colleges of education, and a year later with another college of education. As a result of the mergers it had several sites, two some distance from the main site.

Polytechnic C

Developed on the basis of the advanced work of a former college of technology, the polytechnic has a strong emphasis on science and technology, with faculties of maritime studies, technology, science, business and social science. It has, however, never merged with another institution, and is mainly concentrated on one city-centre site. Its student numbers grew by nearly 70 per cent in the 6 years before the NAB planning exercise, reaching about 4800 FTEs.

Polytechnic D

Polytechnic D was formed from two colleges of technology and a college of art. It operates on a city-centre site, and has four faculties – Art and Design, Engineering, Applied Science and Social Science. Most of its degree courses are sandwich mode and 60 per cent of its 5500 FTE students at the time of the study were in Applied Science and Engineering.

College E

The College is the result of two mergers between three institutions; the first was in 1977, between a college of art and technology and a voluntary college of education, the second in 1983 with a local authority college of education in a nearby town. The resulting college has voluntary status, but with local authority involvement, and financing from both the DES and through the LEA (in a 74:26 ratio), and so at the time of the study was one of our 'hybrid' institutions. The College had about 30 per cent non-advanced work and about 2200 FTE advanced students at the start of the planning exercise, across most NAB programme areas.

College F

College F formally came into existence in 1978 when a new title and articles and a new instrument of government were established by the local authority for an existing technical college. The new College of Higher Education was to have been formed from a merger with a nearby college of education, but this did not take place, and the College exists on a cramped urban site. The College has 2000 full-time and sandwich students and over 4000 part-time students. The areas of study are mainly in business and management, languages, humanities and social sciences on 11 first degree and two masters programmes and on a wide range of professional and vocational courses. An unusual feature is its organization into eight schools in a matrix structure.

College G

This College was formally established in 1983 by merging a college of higher education with the advanced work of a college of technology some distance away. The college of higher education had itself been formed in 1976 by a merger of six colleges of technology, art, commerce, nautical studies and education. At the time of the planning exercise College G had about 2750 advanced FTE students, a large proportion of them on part-time courses.

College H

College H was the smallest of our sample with about 900 FTEs. It was formed in 1977 by a merger of two colleges of education, one maintained, one voluntary to create a 'hybrid' college. The two colleges are maintained as campuses of the institution. Like many former colleges of education, it offers teacher education and 'diversified' courses in the humanities and related areas.

4.4 Data collection and analysis

The framework for data collection and analysis derived from the two basic focuses of the study: the responses adopted by institutional managers and the factors that may be related to them. We saw these related in a kind of matrix structure, a copy of which is shown in Table 4.1. The vertical axis lists possible policy options for the institutions developed in the light of studies of the management of contraction and Davies and Morgan's eclectic paper (1982), and from the logic of the situation faced by institutions at the outset of the NAB exercise. We wished to see whether these options were perceived by institutional managers and which choices were made between them. Were they perceived as alternatives? Did institutions consider 'trade-offs' between them? Did they perceive other options not listed? (Some categories were added to the list during the project.) Against this list we set the range of factors which we considered likely to affect the responses of institutions, covering both their environments and their internal structures and processes.

Table 4.1

Policies	Factors													
	Institutional context					Formal structures of government and management			Management processes			Planning processes		
	Financial history	Relations with LEA	Culture and traditions of the institution	Size, location and concentration of sites	Academic profile	Govern-ment	Manage-ment	Academic structure	Methods of re-source alloca-tion	Political power groupings	Styles of leader-ship	Stages of plan-ning	Infor-mation base	Concep-tual frame-work
1. Strategic policy														
2. Maximizing resources														
3. Maintaining academic profile														
4. Improving efficiency														
5. Personnel policies														
6. Maintaining facilities and support services														
7. Maintaining institutional morale														
8. Improving flexibility														

We are not so naive as to imagine that direct causalities could necessarily be established between the axes of the matrix, nor were we seeking to produce generalizable findings from specific instances, as is so often the intention with case studies. Rather, following our Popperian epistemology, we were seeking to test with some specific cases in particular circumstances some general theories of relationships such as, say, between financial history and present responses to constraint.

Data sources were of three main kinds – interviews, documents and statistics – and they came from two main locations – within the institutions and external to them. Within each case study institution, semi-structured interviews were conducted with the key (usually all) members of the senior management team; this normally included the director or principal, his deputies and assistants, the chief administrative officer, the finance officer and the heads of other central offices. Some of these were interviewed on several occasions. In addition, interviews were conducted with staff at levels in the institution below that of directorate, down to course tutors and rank-and-file teachers. Numbers prevented all staff in these grades from being interviewed; selection was based on the nature of the institution and its problems. For example, in an institution facing cuts in a particular discipline we would seek an interview with the head of that department, but we would also seek an interview with a head of department who did not face heavy cuts to check on alternative problems. Representatives of teacher unions, non-teaching staff unions, and student unions were also interviewed. Although there were occasional initial reluctances, no interview was refused.

Because the circumstances, problems and personalities at each institution varied appreciably, a rigidly consistent interview schedule could not be used, at least not after a certain number of common general questions. What was an issue in one institution or for one respondent may not have been elsewhere or for someone else. The interview was recorded by notes which were later written up, checked with the respondent when they requested this and then indexed (see below). Tape recording was considered but rejected as inhibiting and cumbersome; our prime object was not to accumulate juicy verbatim quotes, but to obtain as clear a statement as possible of the respondent's view of the issues, problems, procedures and consequences of the NAB exercise.

In addition to interviewing individuals, we attended, when possible, numerous meetings of governing bodies, academic boards and their committees as well as informal and other meetings and discussions. These were recorded by notes in a similar way to interviews.

Although we were conscious of the many difficulties, distortions and limitations of interviewing as a means of data collection, it had to be the major source of information, because we were sure that no other approach – questionnaire, observation, etc. – would have yielded sufficient data in the time available or would have permitted a zero non-response rate. One of the reasons for undertaking a large number of interviews was to create an element of 'triangulation' in that the views of the different actors in the institutions' hierarchies could be compared. The use of other kinds of data – observational, documentary and statistical – offered another element of cross-checking.

Documentary material from the institutions consisted of papers, reports, and minutes of academic boards and governing bodies and their various committees and working parties; correspondence with outside bodies such as NAB, CNAA, etc.; and a variety of internal memoranda, bulletins, working papers and administrative documents, as well as less official newsletters, etc. An important source of data about institutions was reports for and on CNAA quinquennial visits. Other documents from outside bodies included audit reports and 'Value for Money' audit documents. The articles and instrument of government and financial regulations of each institution were collected and analysed.

Statistical data collected included student numbers and characteristics, 'performance' indicators such as student:staff ratios, contact hours and class sizes, and the estimates and yearly out-turn expenditure for each institution since the AFE Pool was capped (when available).

External to the institution, interviews were limited to local authority officers and key figures in the NAB and DES. Documents on the NAB exercise from NAB, CNAA and other national bodies were analysed, and statistical and financial data on the public sector as a whole compiled and analysed to describe the context within which the institutions had to operate.

Analysis of data on a project such as this raises not so much methodological problems as administrative. The raw data from each institution comfortably filled a filing drawer, and data on any one topic were scattered throughout interview notes and other material. The solution we adopted was to index all the material. This involved analysing each record for the topics it covered and then recording these, by topic, in a separate index. An interview with a college director might cover each of the policy options and many of the 'factors' on our matrix; statistical data might relate to only one or two headings. In this way a complete catalogue of all the data on each topic was built up for each institution. Given that there were over 20 topics, up to 40 interviews and a vast quantity of other data from each institution, this quickly built up to 1000 or more entries for each institution. Once assembled, the indexes enabled ready identification of all the sources on each topic.

When the case studies were written, a draft was sent to the key figure in the institution, usually the director or a deputy who acted as contact person, for circulation if they wished, comment, and correction of errors of fact or record. Any of the latter were corrected, and preferred phrases inserted where they more accurately reflected events, or spared sensibilities without affecting verisimilitude. In a surprising number of cases, objections were raised to passages or phrases which were derived directly from the institution's own documentation. These were usually dealt with by our quoting verbatim or directly referencing the source. Although views were sometimes expressed that our cases excessively reflected the concern or dislike of some members of the institution for its responses to constraint, in all cases the final case study was agreed by the director or his nominee as a fair account of the management response to the NAB exercise.

References

Cohen, L. and Manion, L. (1985) Research Methods in Education, London: Croom Helm.

Davies, J. L. and Morgan, A. W. (1982) The Politics of Institutional Change. In Wagner, L. (ed.) *Agenda for Institutional Change in Higher Education*. Guildford: SRHE.

5

Strategies in Response to Constraint

5.1 Responses to the NAB planning exercise

We saw in Chapter 3 that as a result of its opposing priorities, NAB sent conflicting signals to institutions and the rules of the game changed in the course of the exercise. In such circumstances, negotiation and direct contact with NAB turned out to be very important for institutions, although the extent to which changes in allocations could be renegotiated was not at all clear at the start. While NAB was involved in deciding policy through its advice on the overall size of the pool, it was also implementing policy through negotiation with institutions and there were considerable changes between preliminary and final allocations for many institutions.

The problems for institutional managers in responding to such conflicting signals were considerable. When we look at the logic of their situations, we can see that the formal stated objectives of the NAB exercise were only one factor to be considered. Institutional managers who were in touch with ongoing developments at NAB and were able to anticipate government decisions proved better equipped to deal with the exercise than those who took NAB's stated objectives at face value.

Another important factor for institutions was their local circumstances, including the recent growth or contraction of student numbers and their relative position in terms of unit costs and other government indicators of 'efficiency'. Their course profile, including the amount of part-time or sub-degree work and the relative proportion of science and technology courses also played an important role. Finally, another factor was the institutions' planning procedures and the extent to which they had developed institutional strategies with agreed aims and future directions for development. NAB asked institutions not only to respond to constraint in terms of student numbers but also to 'prioritize' their work. How their responses to NAB fitted in with their overall institutional strategies will be examined in the next part of this chapter. Here we focus on the process of developing a response to the NAB exercise, the negotiations between NAB and the institutions, culminating in a final allocation in December 1983, and the problems which institutions faced in dealing with the exercise.

When institutions received the planning framework of the NAB exercise on 30

September 1982, they faced two separate but related issues. First, they had to decide how to respond to NAB's request for prioritization. Secondly, they had to decide what student numbers and strategy they wished to adopt with regard to the potential 10 per cent reduction in financial resources. NAB asked institutions to 'judge what balance to strike between maintaining student numbers at lower unit costs, on the one hand, and reducing student numbers on the other' (letter of 26 July 1982). Considering the nature of the NAB exercise, however, the institutions' responses depended not only on the balance between student numbers and resources, but on their judgement of whether they were actually likely to face cuts in resources, and their attitude toward NAB and national planning in general. They had also to decide what extent of consultation with staff was possible or desirable, particularly in the light of the tight timetable.

The decision to prioritize

NAB's request for prioritization presented institutional managers with some difficult problems. In theory, it might be considered good practice to evaluate academic work and decide what areas should have higher priority. In practice, such an exercise might demoralize staff in lower priority areas and cause considerable animosity and competitiveness. In the end, the institution might not actually face a cut in resources or the need to close courses or areas of work. Institutional managers might feel the need to develop contingency plans, but they might not wish to debate them openly within the institution. They had to estimate the risks of refusing to comply with NAB's request against the consequences of open debate about institutional priorities. Alternatively, managers might feel that the NAB exercise provided a good opportunity for an examination of institutional aims and the development of a general consensus on future directions for the institution.

Most of the institutions in our sample decided they did not wish to respond to NAB's request for prioritization by programme areas. Many different justifications were given for this refusal, but a crucial element in this decision was the growing certainty, through communication with other institutions, that most polytechnics and colleges would also refuse to prioritize. For example, College E's academic board originally asked faculties to assess their own priorities and one of its committees to develop appropriate criteria for evaluation. When the faculties reported back in December 1982, there was a general refusal to prioritize and the academic board decided to accept this view since it was by then clear that most other institutions were also going to refuse. While their response to NAB justified this decision on the basis of the lack of provision in the region, the attitude of other institutions and the rumour that institutions which did prioritize were unlikely to be more favourably treated, were clearly important factors.

The general refusal to prioritize on the basis requested by NAB should not imply, however, that institutions rejected the concept of prioritization or did not seriously consider NAB's request. College G, for example, did conduct an extensive evaluation exercise by faculty, but refused to respond in the form provided by NAB, because the NAB programme areas did not fit in with the planning procedures which the College had developed. In their response to NAB, the College made it clear that the NAB request for planning within resource reductions was, in effect, an additional environmental constraint on the internal planning which routinely took place annually.

Other institutions in our sample criticized the form in which NAB required them to respond and the time-frame which they felt would prevent extensive consultation. College F found NAB's programme areas difficult to reconcile with the College's interrelated courses and matrix structure. The Director told the Governing Body that if one area was identified as low priority, it would have a knock-on effect on other subjects and courses and jeopardize the quality of other programmes. He recommended that the College not respond to NAB in the form requested and this decision was supported by the Governing Body and the local authority.

The Academic Board and Governing Body of Polytechnic A was also advised by the Director not to prioritize. They accepted this decision and in their commentary accompanying the NAB forms, they said that NAB had established no universally applicable criteria for the assessment of courses and hoped that NAB would express its own priorities more clearly in the future. They also pointed out the interrelatedness of courses in different programme areas and criticized the hypothetical nature of the exercise, considering the necessity of using out-of-date financial data with the uncertainties about the basis for the pool allocation for 1984–5. Six out of eight of our case study institutions did not prioritize, with most managers deciding it was not worth discussing course closures or loss of staff until their financial situation became clearer. The two institutions which did prioritize did not actually send all the detailed results on to NAB, but the internal exercise turned out to be complex and controversial.

The decision to prioritize internally involved the establishment of criteria for the assessment of courses or areas of work. A general agreement on the aims of the institution might have provided the basis for such an assessment but, in general, as we shall see in Section 5.2, institutions had not previously adopted an agreed statement of their 'mission' or overall aims. Assumptions about the character of the institution often formed the basis for institutional strategies, but they were rarely openly articulated or debated. Whatever the merits of agreeing on a 'mission' for the institution, few managers felt that the NAB exercise provided a good context for such an exercise, considering its assumptions about reductions in resources and the resulting threats to courses and jobs.

The two institutions which decided to prioritize did so for different reasons. One consideration was the extent to which their academic profile fitted in with national priorities. Polytechnic C traditionally emphasized science and technology and management felt that it was in its interest to prioritize. This traditional emphasis, however, had not been openly debated or agreed within the institution. The prioritization exercise had the unintended consequence of lowering the morale of staff in lower priority areas without giving them the opportunity of challenging this emphasis, since decisions on relative priorities were imposed by management. On the other hand, there was a wider dissemination of information than was normally available and more staff became aware of institutional priorities.

The decision of Polytechnic D to undertake a prioritization exercise was made by the Board of Governors and carried out by a special Working Party made up of representatives of governors and management. The plan which was drawn up was intended to demonstrate to NAB the gravity of a 10 per cent reduction in resources in a single year. Some staff saw the Polytechnic's response as an attempt to demonstrate the absurdities of the whole exercise to NAB and did not expect that these contingency plans would actually be implemented if the institution did face a serious cut in resources. Because the institution had low unit costs, a reduction in resources on such a scale would require a reduction in student numbers if academic quality were to be maintained. Therefore, the Working Party reviewed all the institutions' courses and ranked them in terms of seven criteria, including quality, research activity, regional or national needs, student demands, etc. On the basis of these rankings a list of some 20 degree courses was drawn up which would cease intakes in September 1984 to achieve the required savings. This ranking of courses caused considerable controversy and divided the academic community. There were criticisms of the criteria used by the Working Party and the belief that judgements were conditioned by the government's educational philosophy, which explained the low rankings of humanities, arts and social science courses. The prioritization exercise in this institution is vividly recalled by staff 2½ years later as a period of great turmoil, divisiveness and rumour, with lasting consequences for institutional morale.

Decisions on student numbers

The strategy adopted towards student number projections depended to some extent on the institution's assessment of the actual likelihood of having their resources substantially cut. Most managers were unwilling to undertake painful and possibly disruptive discussions on courses for closure and preferred to risk facing the loss of some staff posts and more unfavourable student:staff ratios (SSRs) rather than closing courses and lowering student number targets. With the exception of two of our sample, most institutions tried to maintain their entire academic profiles with as little disruption as possible and requested student number increases or at least stable targets.

The student number targets proposed for 1984–5 depended to a large extent on the institution's previous history of expansion or contraction of student numbers and relative unit costs. Polytechnic C had deliberately expanded student numbers before the NAB exercise, to increase SSRs and lower unit costs. It felt in a strong position with regard to national priorities and proposed a change from its previous expansion to a steady state, without anticipating reductions of staff posts. In contrast, Polytechnic A was not in a strong position with regard to unit costs or SSRs. Faced with the prospect of severe cuts in resources, institutional strategy was to maintain current courses and keep student number targets basically static. If they faced reductions in resources, however, they would have to lose staff posts, which would allow them to retain courses while improving SSRs and unit costs.

The two exceptions were Polytechnics D and B. In line with its prioritization strategy discussed above, Polytechnic D submitted student number targets to NAB for 1984–5 which were considerably below actual student numbers in 1982–3. This strategy was consistent with the intention to demonstrate to NAB the gravity of the effects of a 10 per cent reduction in the AFE Pool allocation all in a single financial year, and with the rejection by the Academic Board and Working Party of the notion of anticipating decisions of NAB by making preliminary cuts in 1983–4.

Polytechnic B was also concerned about the impact of budget reductions in an institution already operating at relatively high SSRs. (Polytechnic D had taken a similar line with the emphasis on its low unit costs.) The strategy developed by the retiring Director involved reductions in student numbers to accommodate a further cut in resources. The Academic Board suggested not merely a general reduction in intakes but also some selective course closures by 1983 and asked each faculty to make proposals. While there was a good deal of resistance to considering course closures, the student targets submitted to NAB involved a slight reduction for 1984–5 and this trend was expected to continue through 1985–6.

The attitude of institutional managers toward government policy played an important part in their basic approach to NAB. Some staff at both Polytechnics B and D felt that their managers had not interpreted the meaning of the NAB exercise correctly. Despite the formal terms calling for a 10 per cent reduction in resources, they felt that resources would follow student numbers and institutions should request higher targets, despite the risk of lowering the unit of resource. In fact, when a new Director took up his appointment at Polytechnic B in the middle of the NAB exercise, he took a radically different approach and negotiated a considerable increase in student numbers with NAB.

Some managers had close contact with what was happening in government and with the various deliberations within NAB. Those with good intelligence about how funding would be allocated by NAB had to decide how far to anticipate government policy and adjust institutional policy in accordance with it. Polytechnic C, which took steps to adjust to national priorities before the NAB exercise, was so far ahead of other institutions that they did not receive the kind of increased allocation which they felt they deserved.

On the other hand, most managers did not feel they could afford to ignore the basis on which their allocation was determined by NAB. There were conflicting signals, for example on NAB's attitude toward part-time work. While NAB asked institutions to consider the special place of part-time work in their response to the exercise, institutions had to consider the difficulty of resourcing such work with the weighting factors used in the allocation of funding to institutions. Both Polytechnics A and B shared this concern.

Preparing the responses to NAB

In addition to deciding on a basic approach to the NAB exercise, institutional managers were faced with the need to establish a procedure for the preparation of their response, including the scope and extent of consultation with staff and the approval of the appropriate internal bodies, such as Academic Boards and Governing Bodies. The decision to prioritize clearly had some impact on this process, since such an exercise was bound to involve a large number of staff, whether they were formally consulted by the decision makers or not. Judgements about the priorities of areas of work were likely to be controversial, especially if the criteria on which they were based were not seen as 'objective' and were not discussed by staff beforehand.

It is revealing that at Polytechnic D, where prioritization caused the most disruption, a special Working Party was set up to rank courses and its findings were challenged by many staff. The publication of the ranking list led to many cases for revised ranking from departments and faculties and complaints of lack of consultation from many individuals. The whole prioritization process was criticized, since it involved subjective criteria and value judgements by individuals about courses with which they were unfamiliar. Critics maintained that achieving a degree of impartiality and objectivity required less hasty consideration, more thorough consultation of documentation, specialist knowledge and informed opinion. The argument for undertaking prioritization was also rejected and these criticisms were not confined to staff from departments whose courses received a low ranking. They maintained that it was unrealistic to try to compare widely different subject areas on anything other than political, as opposed to academic, grounds. Very few courses, it was believed, could be withdrawn on academic grounds in a mature institution enjoying bouyant demand subject to external validation. The lowering of morale in the institutions which decided to prioritize demonstrates the hazards to management of imposing changes in policy without ensuring the support of their staff.

Those institutions which opted for the strategy of maintaining their academic profile with as little disruption as possible varied in the extent to which staff were consulted. They were more likely to use existing machinery to legitimize proposals drafted by management. At the extreme, in College F, which had a history of cuts in funding, the Academic Board refused to participate in resource decisions involving further cuts and gave management a free hand in preparing its response to NAB.

The extent of consultation was limited by an important outside constraint, i.e. the timetable imposed by NAB. Even if special meetings of Academic Boards and their committees were set up by management, the decisions on a basic approach and the drafting of the response tended to be the responsibility of a small group of management and senior staff. The participation of a wider range of staff was limited by the availability of information about the NAB exercise as well as by time. The formal approval of the institutions' responses usually involved only minor amendments to the drafts proposed by management.

Negotiations and allocations

The first response from NAB to the institutions' proposals was a letter dated 26 August 1983, which included the 'indicative allocation' of student numbers and funding for each institution. The final funding allocation depended on further deliberations within NAB and did not reach institutions until December 1983, although it was clear from the indicative allocations that all institutions would not be facing a 10 per cent cut in resources. Student number allocations were based on the institutions' responses to the NAB exercise, which had meanwhile become known as 'bids'. These allocations were the subject of negotiations with NAB in the period between August and December. In some cases, the indicative allocation from NAB was very close to the institution's 'bid' and did not require extensive negotiation. This was true of College G, with the exception of one particular area of work which was under national review by NAB. NAB's acceptance of the College's targets in other areas was seen as confirmation of the trends which it had already planned and which were being implemented before the NAB exercise was undertaken. The most direct impact of NAB was on the small number of staff engaged in the area of work which was closed as a result of NAB's national review.

In cases where NAB had increased student number targets above the level requested by the institutions, this was generally regarded as a good sign, since these institutions expected their final funding allocations to reflect such increases in student numbers. At the extreme was Polytechnic D, which had identified courses for closure and reduced student numbers substantially in its response to NAB. Their indicative allocation gave them 1373 more full-time equivalent students than they had requested! It was also fairly clear from their indicative funding allocation that they would not face a 10 per cent cut in resources, although the Director emphasized to NAB that the indicative allocation would mean a drop in the institution's unit of resource and threaten the quality of work. Polytechnic B's new Director was very disappointed with their indicative allocation, which reflected their original conservative 'bid'. He pointed to the serious effect which the indicative net allocation would have on the Polytechnic's activities in 1984–5 if the implied reduction in funding were implemented. The Polytechnic reviewed its academic profile and accommodation and successfully negotiated a considerable increase in student targets with NAB.

Some institutions got student number targets from NAB below the level they had requested. Polytechnic A received an overall increase in student numbers in its indicative allocation, but this was less than that proposed by the Polytechnic. In addition, the Polytechnic had made some errors in compiling its own targets, which resulted in problems for particular courses or programme areas. The directorate was able to negotiate some increases in targets for particular programme areas which resulted in a final allocation more in line with institutional needs. The final financial allocation, however, involved one of the largest cuts in AFE Pool funding faced by any polytechnic and put the institution in a very serious financial position.

In contrast, in its final allocation, College F received over 100 more students than it had originally requested. The AFE Pool allocation had increased partly because of the increased student numbers, but also as a result of the application of the minimum unit of resource figure to all allocations. As a result of the final allocation, there would be an increase in the College's FTE count of 13 per cent from 1983–4 to 1984–5, and after allowing for increases in fee income and inflation, an unallocated cash addition of £300 000 for the College in 1984–5. While the final allocation justified the Director's expansionist strategy, the indicative allocation had involved considerably less for the College in terms of both student numbers and funding. It had caused considerable concern and prompted a campaign on the part of the Director as well as extensive negotiations with NAB. The final allocation reflected not only these negotiations, but the changes in the funding formula which took place within NAB. Polytechnic C also received more student FTEs than its original bid and a large increase in funding. The Directorate was disappointed in the final funding allocation, however, because they felt that the effect of mitigation meant that the Polytechnic received considerably less of an increase than they deserved, considering their low unit costs.

The constraints of the NAB exercise

This analysis of institutional responses to the NAB exercise highlights the very different approaches taken by the institutions in our sample and the different positions in which they found themselves as a result of the NAB exercise. A number of factors can be identified as crucial to the development of institutional responses. The basic approach by managers depended very much on their local circumstances, on the academic profile and recent history of their institutions, as well as their attitude toward NAB and the extent to which they introduced national priorities into internal decision-making, their assessment of the risk of disruption which might be caused by prioritization, their assessment of the likelihood of actually facing cuts and the extent to which they had intelligence about what was going on within NAB and the government.

The procedures adopted to prepare their responses depended on the scope and extent of consultation desired by managers, which was influenced by their basic approach to the NAB exercise, the availability of information to staff and the tight timetable imposed by NAB. The experience of the two institutions in our sample which decided to prioritize suggests that the determination of institutional priorities without an agreement on the general aims of the institution or the criteria on which work should be judged can prove harmful to staff morale. It also suggests that the NAB exercise did not provide a good opportunity for an examination of institutional aims or the development of a general consensus on future directions for the institutions.

The NAB exercise did not create a situation whose logic encouraged institutions to plan strategically. One of the major problems was the changing rules of the game. Institutions were asked for plans on the basis of a hypothetical 10 per cent cut in resources and then these plans were treated as bids in an allocation based on different financial circumstances. We should record, however, that all of our institutions recognized the importance of their proposals: they did not argue, as others did, that they did not realize the implications of them – even the hybrid colleges, new to the NAB process, recognized their future was at stake and spent considerable effort in arguing their cases both in their formal responses and subsequently.

The alternatives offered to institutions at the outset of the exercise – of planning for higher student numbers at a reduced unit of resource, or fewer students – soon became irrelevant. The 1984–5 allocation was based on higher student numbers at a reduced unit of resource. Institutions which took the first option seriously (such as Polytechnics B and D) and proposed reduced numbers found they were given increased numbers regardless, though one of these institutions had realized the way things were developing and later argued for increased targets: '[the Director and Management] tried to anticipate what NAB would decide – student numbers to be cut. Then student numbers were tied to funding, which was detrimental.' All this helped to engender both a feeling of disbelief about the exercise, similar to that which has been reported by others (Davies and Morgan 1982), and also a sense of futility: why go through all this if NAB simply allocates a set of targets anyway? The disparity between the 'indicative' and final allocations in many of our institutions added to the sense of futility and irritation about the nature of the exercise.

The sense of futility was heightened for at least one of our institutions by the effects of the allocation methodology eventually chosen. Although this institution was highly 'efficient' after its policy of 'turning up the burner' and received a 10 per cent increase in Pool allocation as a result of the exercise, it felt that it had been allocated less than it would have been entitled to if 'mitigation' and 'moderation' had not been applied to protect more expensive institutions. In this case it could be argued that by over-zealously anticipating government policy, the institution had penalized itself: it could have anticipated that some damping mechanism would continue to be employed in Pool allocations and might have fared just as well at less cost to itself. The allocation system penalized those who conformed closest to its criteria. The position of Polytechnic C contrasted with that of College F which also anticipated the outcome of the exercise, but received additional resources because it had historically been starved of them.

Many of our institutions reported that the timing of the exercise meant that adequate consideration was not always possible in preparing their responses: several institutions submitted returns with what were eventually recognized as errors and one institution (partly also because of the inadequacy of its data base) had considerable difficult in responding in the time available with an accurate statistical return. But these problems paled somewhat in comparison to the changing nature of the exercise. Institutions struggled to predict the consequences of each of the funding mechanisms considered by NAB between August and December 1983. The choice was crucial. At Polytechnic A the Director felt that the indicative allocation was so inadequate as to threaten its existence. He described the difficulty of planning in such an environment as 'playing football when someone changes the rules every five minutes'. When the allocation was determined, it meant that planning for the 1984–5 budget could not take place until January 1984.

Other features of the planning exercise and allocation caused concern in institutions. The definition of programme areas was a problem in several. Institutions with multi-disciplinary courses or modular courses covering several programme areas had difficulties in allocating enrolments to the correct programmes, with expensive consequences if the allocation was to a low weighted area. At College H students on a Related Arts course were classified in the humanities programme area rather than the much higher weighted performing arts programme (a mistake eventually rectified by NAB). The same college reported that the classification of programmes complicated its plans to 'package' several courses for more efficient operation because reductions in targets in one programme area may have knock-on effects in others. Polytechnic A was concerned at the classification of psychology not as a science but as part of programme J, Social and Administrative Studies, because its course was clinically oriented and a 12:1 SSR was inappropriate. Polytechnic C found that its Staff Schedules Analysis (SSA) system was incompatible with NAB programme areas. The system of target student enrolments also presented problems. Most institutions were concerned that new course developments could only take place by replacement of an existing course, even if there was evident demand for both courses. College H, for example, found that a proposed MA course could be developed only if enrolments in other courses in the programme areas were reduced. Most of our institutions, in the period between the indicative and final allocations, negotiated successfully with NAB to adjust their targets, but several institutions faced with what they felt were low targets decided to positively over-recruit. College H recruited some 9 per cent of students in excess of its NAB target. Polytechnic A, because it had 'underbid' in the planning exercise, adopted a policy of recruiting some 7.4 per cent over NAB targets.

Some institutions expressed concern about the system of funding for research. Holding back a small proportion of the Pool for research was seen by staff concerned with research at Polytechnic C as offering an opportunity for detailed control over the kind of research funded and involving time-consuming application procedures. This was compounded by the feeling that the funds involved were inadequate. One Reader claimed that his research fulfilled all the criteria outlined by NAB for applicability and links with industry but was not funded because it was in social sciences not science and technology! Staff at Polytechnic B were worried that selectivity would mean funds going only to the already strong, preventing the development of research elsewhere.

Other, more technical problems arose from the allocation methodology, affecting institutions to varying extents. They have been explored in detail by O'Hara (1985). The problems concerned the construction of programme weights, allowances for London Weighting and central establishment charges, catering and residence elements and the treatment of fee income. As we saw in

Chapter 3, the DES recognized that the weightings were very sensitive to changes in the assumptions about relative student numbers or the division of expenditure (between teaching and non-teaching costs and within the latter) used. The historic student number data used for calculating the programme weights was significantly different from those used in the actual distribution, so that institutions which would have benefited had the actual student number distribution been used did not.

The calculation of the London Weighting allowance ignored variations in the pattern of spending in institutions between teaching and non-teaching costs so that some institutions (Polytechnic A among them) were penalized in comparison to others. Similarly, the flat percentage allowance for central establishment charges bore no relationship to actual changes, so that some of our institutions received considerably more generous allocations than others. There was similarly little relationship between catering and residence allowances and actual expenditure on these items. On fees NAB calculated a notional income for institutions (to make net allocations from the AFE Pool) based on historic patterns of enrolment, and not those in its target student numbers. As a result some institutions received more fee income than assumed while others received less.

The nature of NAB and its funding mechanisms was criticized more generally by managers and staff in several of our institutions. They were concerned, for example, that the funding mechanism prevented innovation. At College H, for example, the Director had presented a paper to his Academic Board in 1983 criticizing 'the tendency to centralise' and the 'out-of-date over simple view' of the (similar) funding mechanism which appeared to use large city-based institutions as a yardstick. In his view the needs of smaller non-metropolitan colleges (like his own) tended to get neglected. These might be 'the most innovative and change directed' institutions, yet 'these are precisely the institutions heavily squeezed by the policies of the agencies that also aim to promote change and to open up access'.

Fears about the nature of NAB as an agent of central government were expressed. The responses from Polytechnic B are typical. Some staff saw the advent of NAB as a change from 'bottom up to top down' planning; many saw it as remote and alien, and hence increasing the level of uncertainty within the Polytechnic, and it was widely felt that it was a 'centrist organization' and a 'tool of the DES'. But there was also recognition of the potential benefits of a rationally planned sector, with NAB as its champion.

The benefits of NAB were also seen at some institutions in terms of their relationship with their local authorities. College F felt that the planning exercise had created a greater awareness in the authority of the College's role and problems, and the AFE Pool allocation was now seen as specific income attributed to the College, though this has the disadvantage that authority members are thought to regard the College's funds as fixed and that any new proposal has to be financed out of existing resources. But the emphasis on the College's 'own' resources is felt to give it greater discretion and control over its affairs than it had in the past.

The 'hybrid' colleges

For the hybrid colleges, the constraints of the NAB system of funding were compounded by the fact that part of their funds were received under the direct grant arrangements of the DES for teacher education. By the time they took part in the NAB planning exercise the colleges had already suffered from cuts in their DES grants and were anxious that they were not to be cut twice. The response to NAB from College H emphasized that it had undergone a cut of the order of 10 per cent over the previous 2 years and did not wish to do so again. For this College the point was crucial since five-ninths of its funding came from DES, while at College G the figure was only 16 per cent.

The direct grant arrangements were themselves complicated, involving the colleges in submitting estimates and accounts in a specified format to the Department and, like the AFE Pool, arrangements had been subject to change. College H had decided to privatize its catering and residence facilities in response to a change in funding arrangements for these items and its management expressed concern that further changes in grant regulations for standard charges and capital items would add to their burden of administration, while changes in the control of expenditure by DES to gross expenditure were seen as constraining the College's development by reducing incentives to raise income. There were complaints too about the complexity of the regulations and accounting requirements, though it must be said that all these views were set in the context of the recognition of the sympathetic treatment the college in general felt that it had received from the Department.

The transition to the NAB system caused problems for the voluntary colleges since it involved changes in the basis upon which FTE calculations were made. College H claimed that it was no longer able to secure funding for courses it ran in social work because they were non-poolable and so neither the AFE Pool nor DES funding calculated upon it was available. Similarly, the College reported that students on school-based in-service education did not produce registered FTEs and were thus not financially supported.

The hybrid colleges, however, were able to point to the benefits of their voluntary status. We have already seen the formal freedoms that they possessed over financial and staffing matters that were not available to the maintained colleges. These very real powers are recognized by the managements of the colleges, as are their powers to spend from their trust funds on approved items. There are benefits also resulting from their status as charities, though as voluntary colleges they are liable to VAT in a way that maintained colleges are not, and a manager in one of the colleges has calculated that the losses here outweigh the gains.

Problems of planning under NAB

Many of the criticisms of the planning exercise have, of course, been acknowledged by NAB, and the lessons incorporated by amendments to NAB procedures and funding mechanisms, although this was of no use to institutions at the time of the planning exercise. At base, however, many of them challenge the fundamental nature of NAB planning and resource allocation. The paradoxes and conflicts that our institutions variously reported they were presented with include: the difficulty of planning within short-term funding ·horizons and changing funding mechanisms; the direct local consequences of a national funding methodology; the difficulty of responding to demand and creating new courses within a system of student number targets; and the problems of maintaining content, quality and innovation with restricted resources.

But so long as the principles of unit funding and target student numbers are employed, institutions will continue to face what they rightly or wrongly regard as paradoxes, conflicting signals, and constraints on their capacity to respond to demand for their courses and to respond to financial constraint.

5.2 Institutional strategies

Although the NAB exercise did not prove a good opportunity for institutions to discuss long-term goals, their ability to respond did depend to some extent on their planning procedures and the existence of overall aims which had been agreed before the exercise began. When we widen the focus of our analysis beyond the NAB exercise itself, we find that institutions faced financial constraint in the whole period leading up to the NAB exercise and the ability of institutions to cope depended not only on their local circumstances but also on their strategic capabilities.

The literature examining the response of institutions to financial constraint suggests the importance of long-term goals and the development of specific objectives and aims. The Jarratt Report, for example, found no corporate strategic plans which were regularly reviewed and updated by the universities it examined, with only limited forward planning 'at the margin' (CVCP 1985, p. 17). Its recommendations included 'developing a rolling academic and institutional plan, which will be reviewed regularly and against which resources will be allocated' (CVCP 1985, p. 36). This stress on the importance of long-term strategy is shared by Sims (1982), Fielden (1982) and Sizer (1982).

In their discussion of internal decision-making in universities, Shattock and Rigby (1983) noted a lack of coordination between academic planning and resource allocation and pointed out that

> resource allocation implies the existence of institutional objectives, whether embodied in an academic plan, or in decisions of Senate and Council, or enshrined in some intangible way in charters and statutes. (Shattock and Rigby 1983, p. 53)

In fact, the literature suggests that there are few examples of the kind of formal 'mission statement' discussing long-term goals and objectives in British universities and our findings confirm that this is also true for public sector institutions. What we did find was that many colleges and polytechnics did have some sense of institutional priorities which guided decision-making and the choice of policies, but this was rarely in the form of a formal document discussed and approved by the institution as a whole.

An ideal-type model of strategic planning would require long-term planning based on a 'mission statement'. Most of the literature stresses the need for long-term planning, as opposed to the kind of crisis management which often emerges from last minute cuts in funding or even goals which only look ahead 2 or 3 years. For example, Sims maintains that

> whatever the difficulties of the time it is essential that the university should have some form of strategic plan. During the last few years it has often been the case that the need to react pragmatically to new financial limitations has largely obscured longer term goals. (Sims 1972, p. 168)

This emphasis on the longer term implies a sense of future direction for the institution and the identification of areas which have potential for expansion, along with those where demand has dropped. Considering the lead time necessary for course development and the difficulties involved in moving out of less attractive areas, the longer term nature of this kind of planning becomes clear.

There is little doubt that the size of the cuts faced by some institutions meant that managers had little choice but to resort to crisis management. In other cases, however, their freedom to manoeuvre was considerably wider and the logic of their situation called for strategic planning. The avoidance of crisis management requires planning mechanisms which allow both flexible responses to changing circumstances and the chance for an examination of the consequences of the strategy adopted. Such planning mechanisms only work if the institution has adopted clear long-term goals against which immediate policies can be evaluated.

When 'mission statements' are discussed, many people think this means a detailed elaborate document outlining everything the institution will do for the next 10 years or more. The turbulent environment, however, militates against such exact predictions and we are arguing that 'mission' should mean a sense of the problems they are trying to solve, rather than a listing of the activities that they currently or propose to undertake. Mission in this sense means the institutions see themselves as the solution to problems located in their environment – locally, regionally and nationally. Mission statements, then, first define the problems which institutions are trying to solve and, secondly discuss the solutions which are proposed to tackle them. In different circumstances, different solutions may be appropriate or necessary, because new constraints may rule some out or allow previously rejected solutions to be adopted.

In order for such a sense of 'mission' to contribute to strategic planning, it has to be based on consensus. If the goals of the mission statement are discussed democratically throughout the institution, then strategies developed to deal with financial constraint are more likely to generate consensus. Bodies responsible for planning will then be able to evaluate policies on the basis of agreed

goals and they can provide the necessary forum for discussion of the consequences of changing institutional strategies.

When we examine the formal documents adopted by our case study institutions, we find little resemblance to this ideal-type mission statement. The one
institution which came closest to having this type of mission statement did not
discuss relative priorities and the one which identified priority areas did not
agree them throughout the institution.

Many institutions do adopt formal statements, either through the Academic
Board or Governing Body, which discuss aims and objectives. These statements
are sometimes drawn up in response to a quinquennial visit from the CNAA or a
planning document from a government body. The common problem with these
kinds of statements is that they tend to reinforce the *status quo* rather than
providing the basis for future planning. As the Jarratt Report said:

> Objectives and aims in universities are defined only in very broad terms.
> They usually take the form of general statements of intent to maintain and
> improve the quality of teaching and research across all subjects at present
> established in the institutions. (CVCP 1985, p. 17)

In three of our case study institutions, however, general statements of
principles did have some influence on institutional strategy and provided clues
to relative priorities. Polytechnics C and D both mentioned their traditional
commitment to particular areas of study and the importance of such subjects for
their contribution to the local community or region. These were also the only
two institutions in our sample which did undertake the prioritization requested
by NAB, although the details were not necessarily actually sent to NAB. Their
general statements of commitment, however, did not explicitly give priority to
these particular areas, although they may have underlain some of the assumptions of the Directorate in developing institutional strategies to deal with
financial constraint. Since specific priorities had not been openly discussed or
approved by the institution as a whole, however, they could not provide the
basis for consensus on how to deal with NAB's request for prioritization.

In Polytechnic C the process of prioritization was controlled and imposed by
the Directorate, while in Polytechnic D it was handled by a special Working
Party made up of Governing Body representatives. In both cases the prioritization had the effect of heightening the specificity of the general statements, by
not only confirming but emphasizing the relative importance of the subject
areas mentioned and thus causing considerable controversy and resentment,
particularly in areas which were now openly identified as of lower priority.

While the formal adoption of mission statements might be time-consuming
and difficult, it has the advantage of providing a basis for consensus throughout
the institution on future directions. In a period of financial contraction, formal
statements may be useful in identifying relative priorities, but only if they
discuss specific priorities and have been debated and adopted by the appropriate representative bodies. The extent to which statements discuss specific
priorities and future directions points to another aspect of institutional strategy
which relates to its scope and content.

As we have seen, statements can refer to very broad general principles, emphasize relative priorities or discuss specific aspects of an institution's academic profile. Of the three institutions which adopted general statements of aims and objectives Polytechnics A and D came closest to some form of formal 'mission statement'. They both emphasized access to local students, including non-traditional or mature students, and service to the local community. This commitment involved the provision of a wide range of modes and levels of study as well as innovative course structures and did influence academic planning within these institutions, since it related to specific aspects of their academic profile. However, while these statements did point to specific needs in the local community which these institutions were making a special effort to satisfy, they did not discuss relative priorities or specific objectives for future development. As a result, they provided little guidance on how to deal with financial constraint, and in fact these two institutions reacted very differently to the NAB exercise. Polytechnic D demonstrated that the 10 per cent reduction in resources assumed by NAB would require reductions in student numbers and the possible closure of courses or areas of study. In contrast, Polytechnic A was determined to protect its entire academic profile and requested slightly more students from NAB.

The scope of institutional strategies is not necessarily limited to formal statements, however, and may involve assumptions based on the historical traditions and character of institutions which are not explicitly discussed. These underlying assumptions may prove more influential in responding to financial constraint than general statements of principle. Davies and Morgan point out that such 'core values' can play an important part in arriving at a consensus on institutional priorities, which is difficult in a crisis period (1982, pp. 174–6).

College H traditionally stressed a student-centred approach to education and a major aspect of its institutional strategy was an innovative restructuring of courses designed to provide flexibility and reduce costs. Polytechnic C and College G were geographically isolated in regions relatively underprovided in terms of higher education. Both stressed their regional contribution and emphasized expansion of student numbers, despite financial constraint. College F also emphasized growth and had relied on the generation of income from overseas students and special courses to cope with reductions in public funds, as well as putting up with increasing strains caused by overcrowding of facilities.

The objectives of institutional strategies can range from extensive discussions of academic values to relatively straightforward goals such as moving from college to polytechnic or polytechnic to university status. The three institutions who emphasized expansion (Polytechnic C and Colleges F and G) as well College E shared aspirations for status. As well as providing a goal capable of mobilizing staff and students and developing consensus, this kind of goal also has an impact on institutional policies. Such goals are often based on assessments of areas of work which are seen as 'centres of excellence' or the contribution of an institution in a particular region or community. As a result, institutional strategies often emphasize improving quality, and areas such as staff development and research may become 'sacred cows', i.e. areas to be protected from cuts.

Polytechnic C, with the encouragement and assistance of its local authority, put considerable emphasis on generating research, attracting outside research funding and bringing in highly qualified staff. The titles of academic staff were also revised to include a professorate. While the staff of this institution seemed to be proud of their research record and supported aspirations for status, these kinds of goals do not necessarily generate consensus. At College F the Director wished to improve quality by bringing in highly qualified staff at a senior level. This initiative was strongly opposed by many staff, who felt that financial pressures had put considerable strain on teaching resources and, if there was investment in support of teaching staff, they themselves would have the time to play the kind of role envisaged by the Director for these new senior staff. Some staff expressed misgivings about this emphasis on research, since they felt that the institution's reputation was based much more on the quality of its teaching and this was a more appropriate focus. Most institutions sought to maintain and improve the quality of courses by reviewing and revising their processes to evaluate and monitor courses.

The popularity of institutional strategies involving aspirations for status can be related directly to the funding bases for different types of institutions. Colleges often emphasized the advantages which polytechnics gained in terms of funding, while polytechnics were quick to emphasize the difference in the unit of resource across the binary line. Beyond the goal of improving status, however, institutional strategies rarely included an assessment of the resource implications of institutional policies and goals. Sizer (1982) emphasized that managers should motivate institutions 'to examine systematically the future environment in which it will be operating and to identify threats and opportunities' and 'to evaluate the institution's current subject area portfolio and critical resources' (Sizer 1982, p. 64). Institutional strategies in our case studies usually included specific policies in areas such as the levels of staffing or SSRs, but these policies were not usually related to overall aims, specific objectives for the future, or assessments of current programmes. Most of the assessments of institutional performance were related to external constraints rather than internal goals.

If we compare the actual planning procedures of our case study institutions with our ideal-type model of strategic planning, we find a pattern which is far removed from the 'rolling academic and institutional plan, which will be reviewed regularly and against which resources will be allocated' as envisaged by the Jarratt Report. More commonly, institutional policies were guided by underlying assumptions about the character and traditions of the institution and the Directorate's assessment of their position in terms of national priorities and standard indicators. For example, in the two institutions which emphasized particular subject areas and prioritized as part of the NAB exercise, the favoured areas were science and technology, which had been emphasized in government policy. In fact, in the three institutions which emphasized growth despite financial constraint, the Directorates saw their institutions as congruent with national priorities and therefore unlikely to actually face cuts.

This congruence was not just related to favoured subject areas, since College F did not, in fact, have any courses in science and technology. It was in this case related to external concern for 'efficiency', particularly unit costs and SSR levels. Some institutional managers saw these external assessments as critical factors in the development of their institutional strategies. Polytechnic C introduced a policy of increasing student numbers before the NAB exercise in order to increase SSR levels and improve 'efficiency'. Polytechnics B and D also emphasized their efficiency by 'running a tight ship' and not always filling vacant posts. There was an increasing use of standard indicators, particularly SSRs, in the assessment of staffing levels and the allocation of resources.

As we shall discuss in Chapter 6, most institutions used the HMI/NAB best-practice SSRs in resource allocation to some extent because, first of all, external assessment of their 'efficiency' was felt to be seen in terms of these performance indicators. Secondly, the development of internal performance indicators proved extremely difficult in periods of financial constraint. While authors such as Sizer or the Jarratt Committee emphasize the need for internal performance indicators and the importance of periodic performance assessments, their development involves long lead times. As Davies and Morgan point out, conducting evaluations and reviews in a highly charged political environment gives rise to both offensive and defensive evaluation strategies and tactics. It can lead to suspicions of hidden agendas and criticism of the criteria used in the assessments (Davies and Morgan 1982, p. 174). The two institutions which did prioritize faced these very problems and experienced a lowering of morale or disruption, despite the fact that they did not face a serious loss of funds, and even eventually received additional income.

If an institution had its own internal aims, but these were not in line with government priorities, it was in a difficult position, although possibly better able to mobilize staff in support of institutional goals than an institution without agreed aims. Polytechnic A was one institution with some form of mission statement and it emphasized a commitment to providing access to non-traditional students, so the institution relied heavily on part-time courses, which it saw as unfavourably resourced. While NAB stressed the importance of part-time work and urged its protection, this institution claimed it had to subsidize it by mixing modes of study and allowing full-time courses to support part-time ones. This institution was also unfavourably placed in terms of SSR levels and unit costs. The Directorate found the use of HMI/NAB SSRs in internal assessments of staffing levels to be quicker and less controversial than trying to develop its own performance indicators. The Director's institutional strategy was based on the need to get the institution more in line with other institutions in order to avoid the very serious cuts in funding which the institution had been facing and continued to face.

Most of our case study institutions, however, did not have mission statements and lacked overall strategies. Most tended to react conservatively to financial constraint by protecting their current activities. Most institutions did not have experience of extensive performance reviews and had not previously agreed criteria for evaluation or internal performance indicators. Even those institutions which did prioritize did not go back to a basic discussion of long-term goals and the prioritization tended to reinforce existing, if not openly acknowledged, priorities.

In the absence of agreed goals and internal performance indicators, most managers tended to evaluate their institution in terms of outside indicators of 'efficiency'. They introduced policies designed to increase management in-formation about SSRs and teaching loads and to increase management control of finances. As we shall discuss in more detail in Chapter 6, most managers decided to take what we have described as the 'efficiency option'.

The focus of most policies to improve efficiency related to changes in procedures for resource allocation and personnel policies. Considering the proportion of spending on staff, it is not surprising that personnel policies became a critical element in institutional strategies, with most institutions in-troducing policies designed to move to the overall 12:1 SSR recommended by NAB. Some institutions decided it was necessary to reduce the number of staff (Polytechnic A and Colleges E and H) while others relied on increased student numbers to bring up overall SSRs (Polytechnic C and Colleges F and G). Some institutions also relied on policies designed to make saving on non-staff costs to improve efficiency. Managers attempted to reorganize sites or find savings at all levels of expenditure, including the use of telephones, travel budgets or catering expenses. College H 'privatized' its catering and residence facilities, using private contractors to manage them.

Most of these policies to improve efficiency involved serious trade-offs for the institutions. Where SSRs were raised, class sizes usually went up and teaching staff had less time for course development work or research. Where sites were lost, students and staff had to travel longer distances and one institution lost part of its regional role. In two institutions which relied on student number increases, facilities tended to become overcrowded and support services were strained. The implications of taking the 'efficiency option' will be analysed in more detail in Section 6.3.

Many institutions also began to emphasize income generation as an im-portant means of offsetting the loss of public funds. The commitment of institutional managers to such policies depended on the Directorate's estima-tion of the potential demand for such activities in their area, and their relation to the core activities of the institution. Polytechnic C saw research activity as critical to its own internal goals and was able to encourage the attraction of considerable outside research support. In contrast, College H did not feel that such activities were always integral to its educational goals and preferred to see income-generating activities, such as conferences, taking place out of term under the control of outside contractors. There is a wide range of possible income-generating activities, however, and most institutional strategies in-volved at least the consideration of the most appropriate forms and the incentives which were required to generate such activity.

Despite the common concern with improving efficiency, the most striking feature of the institutional strategies adopted by our case study institutions is their variety. These differences are clearly related to the particular circumstances faced by each institution. The previous history of each institution played an important part in determining, for example, whether to adopt a strategy of cutting student numbers or losing staff to deal with reductions in resources. Polytechnic A felt that a strategy of shedding staff was the only possible one, since closing courses would only lead to fewer students and less funding, without improving the institution's unit costs, which were high in comparison with other institutions. College F was in a favourable geographic location to attract students for special courses and was able to emphasize income generation as an important part of its institutional strategy. To the extent which managers felt their institutions to be congruent with national priorities, they were able to take positive expansionist policies despite financial constraint. Finally, the actual level of funding reductions faced by the institutions varied widely and had a crucial impact on the strategies adopted in the period of our study.

References

Committee of Vice Chancellors and Principles (CVCP) (1985) *Report of the Steering Committee for Efficiency Studies in Universities*. CVCP.

Davies, J. L. and Morgan, A. W. (1982) The Politics of Institutional Change. In Wagner, L. (ed.) *Agenda for Institutional Change in Higher Education*. Guildford: SRHE.

Fielden, J. (1982) Strategies for Survival. In Morris, A. and Sizer, J. (eds) *Resources and Higher Education*. Guildford: SRHE.

O'Hara, R. (1985) Avoiding the Unavoidable – Formula Funding and Institutional Costs in PSHE. CIS Commentary 29, North East London Polytechnic.

Shattock, M. and Rigby, G. (eds) (1983) *Resource Allocation in British Universities*. Guildford: SRHE.

Sims, G. (1982) Resource Allocation Within Universities. In Morris, A. and Sizer, J. (eds) *Resources and Higher Education*. Guildford: SRHE.

Sizer, J. (1982) Assessing Institutional Performance and Progress. In Wagner, L. (ed.) *Agenda for Institutional Change in Higher Education*. Guildford: SRHE.

6

Efficiency and Education

In this chapter we look at the way in which our case study institutions responded to the imperatives to control expenditure and increase efficiency of the NAB planning exercise. In Section 6.1 we look at the way 'efficiency' was interpreted in terms of resource allocation and patterns of spending, the extent to which mechanisms of resource allocation and control were used by institutions to respond to constraint, and how these mechanisms in turn affected their responses. In Section 6.2 we examine the development of academic policies and the kind of structural changes introduced in response to financial constraint. The educational implications of policies for resource allocation and control and academic planning are then discussed in the final section of this chapter.

6.1 Resource allocation and control

The underlying imperatives of the NAB planning exercise were unambiguous. The government's intentions were to reduce expenditure in real terms per student, rationalize provision and increase efficiency.

The need to reduce unit costs and improve SSRs had been articulated well before the exercise. In February 1981, for example, the then Secretary of State had noted that the student:staff ratio was 7:1, that current expenditure plans were for a decrease in resources in the coming year, but that there was scope for reducing student unit costs and that he expected the main economies to be secured in that way (DES Press Release, 25 February 1981). The 1982 Expenditure White Paper confirmed the picture: expenditure on higher education was to fall by at least 10 per cent in real terms between 1980–1 and 1984–5. It was in this context of a continued reduction in spending and an increase in efficiency that the NAB planning exercise began.

The NAB letter of 26 July 1982 was set out in the opening paragraph of the 1982 White Paper on reduced spending on higher education, and explained that 'on reasonable assumptions about pay and price increases, institutions' expenditure . . . will fall on average by about 10 per cent in real terms between 1982–83 and 1983–84'. The planning exercise was NAB's response to this scenario.

The July letter appeared to offer institutions a choice of ways of meeting the requirement to reduce their spending by this amount. In the event, the issue was largely determined in the planning exercise by the decision to increase total student numbers at a lower overall unit of resource.

The message for most institutions was clear. Their total Pool income could be maintained only if student numbers were high; this in turn meant that overall student:staff ratios would have to rise and costs per student would fall. In so far as these are measures of it, 'efficiency' would have to increase.

Institutional responses

Institutions could not afford to ignore these imperatives and all their strategies recognized to a greater or lesser extent the need for efficiency. While the actual meaning of efficiency was interpreted differently in different institutions, managers became increasingly concerned with student:staff ratios, and all our institutions showed upwards movements in these, both in the period since the capping of the Pool and in direct response to the NAB exercise. To achieve these changes, particularly at the time of the planning exercise, managers looked increasingly at the control of resources, teaching loads and performance measures. New systems of resource allocation needed to be developed in some institutions to implement these policies of increased control, while in others new accounting procedures were introduced.

However, the ways in which individual institutions responded varied considerably. In large part, this variation reflected their circumstances at the time of the NAB exercise. This, in turn, reflected their previous histories, and in particular the extent to which they had already been subject to and responded to constraint and to which they had anticipated the nature of the constraints of the NAB exercise.

Thus, while the need to achieve SSRs consistent with NAB's overall target of 12:1 for the sector was recognized in all our case study institutions, the extent and timing of this achievement varied considerably and the acceptance of such a target had quite different consequences in different institutions. Not all institutions could or were prepared to immediately reach the overall 12:1 sector target proposed by NAB. The target was too far removed from their present position.

Student:staff ratios

Before we look at data on student:staff ratios, we need to make some observations about them. Our analysis is based on data returned by the institutions to the Pooling Committee as part of its annual spring monitoring survey. This has been undertaken since 1972–3 by the DES on behalf of the Pooling Committee in the spring term of each year. However, the sample of institutions on which the survey has been based has increased since its inception, as has the response rate, and the classification of the courses covered has changed from advanced and

non-advanced to poolable and non-poolable; all this means that strict comparability of the figures between years cannot be guaranteed. Equally, the survey
relies on the reliability of the data returned to the Committee by the colleges.
These reservations notwithstanding some useful analysis can be made of the
pattern of changes in our case study institutions.

The trend in SSRs in PSHE as a whole had been upwards since the capping of
the AFE Pool in 1979–80 (and mostly indeed since before that). For example, in
polytechnics the overall SSRs for advanced work had increased from 8.3 in
1979–80 to 11.9 (within a whisker of the NAB target of 12) by 1984–5. In other
colleges the increase was somewhat less; the major colleges of further education
in 1979–80 had an overall SSR for advanced work of 7.9; by 1984–5 the figure
for major establishments (other than polytechnics) was 10.5, and for minor
establishments 8.6.

Our case study institutions had, in the main, reflected the national trend in
student:staff ratios. The four polytechnics in our sample had increased their
SSRs in all three faculty groups in the period since the capping of the AFE Pool
(see Figures 6.1 to 6.3). Three of the four had begun the period with SSRs mostly
above the average for polytechnics; of these three, only Polytechnic D had a
figure (for art and design) below the average for polytechnics. At Polytechnic A,
however, all three 1979–80 figures were below the average.

Increases in SSRs were on occasion a little erratic, with reverses in some
years, but the overall trend was upward. Marked increases are found in some

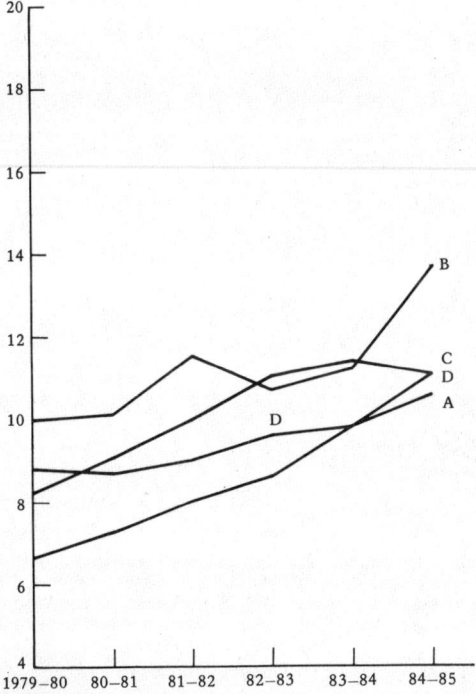

Figure 6.1   SSRs Polytechnics
Group 1 (Poolable)

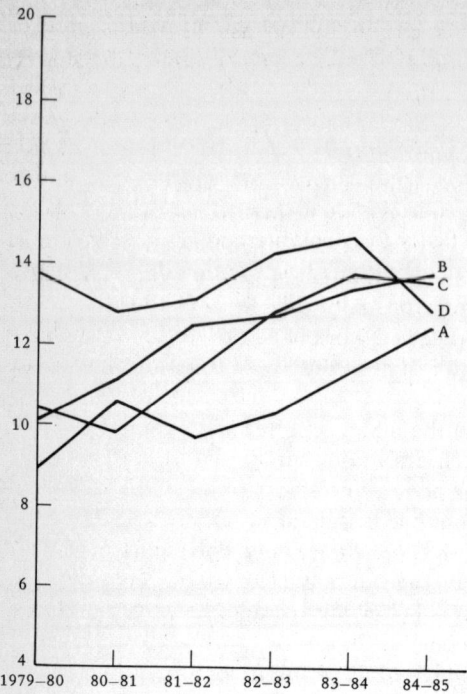

Figure 6.2   SSRs Polytechnics
Group 2 (Poolable)

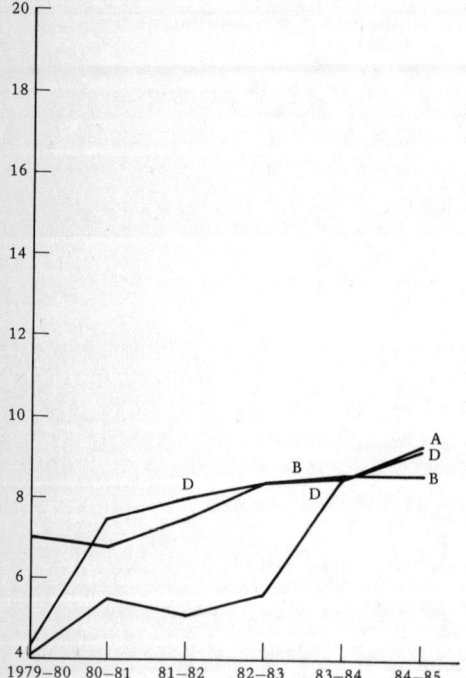

Figure 6.3   SSRs Polytechnics Art
and Design (Poolable)

cases. Polytechnic A more than doubled its SSR in Art and Design by 1983–4 from (the admittedly low) 4.1 to 8.5 and in Group 2 faculties increased it from 8.9 to 11.4.

Among the colleges in our sample, the pattern was similar, though fewer data are available for these institutions since College H was involved in the Pooling Committee survey for only 2 years and data for two other colleges were not retrievable because of the loss of the codes for their constituent colleges by the DES! Nevertheless, it is clear that SSRs for poolable courses had generally moved upwards, reflecting the pattern for major colleges nationally (see Figures 6.4 to 6.6). The most marked increases were from an SSR of 4.8 in Group 1 at College F to 10.3 by 1983–4. There were some declines notably in Group 1 at College H. Overall, reflecting college SSRs nationally our colleges had lower SSRs than the polytechnics.

Student numbers

Student:staff ratios are of course the relationship between two figures, student and staff numbers. They may be increased by increasing the former and/or decreasing the latter. Since the capping of the Pool, our case study institutions mostly adopted at least the first option. For our polytechnics, the period since 1979–80 had been one of growth of student numbers, though the extent to which

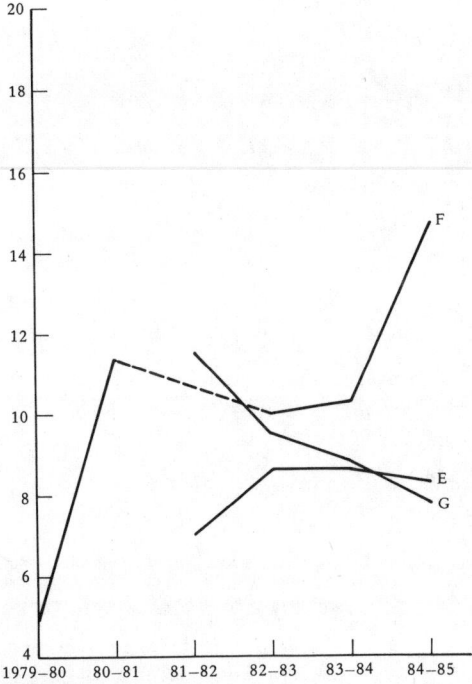

Figure 6.4 SSRs Colleges Group 1 (Poolable)

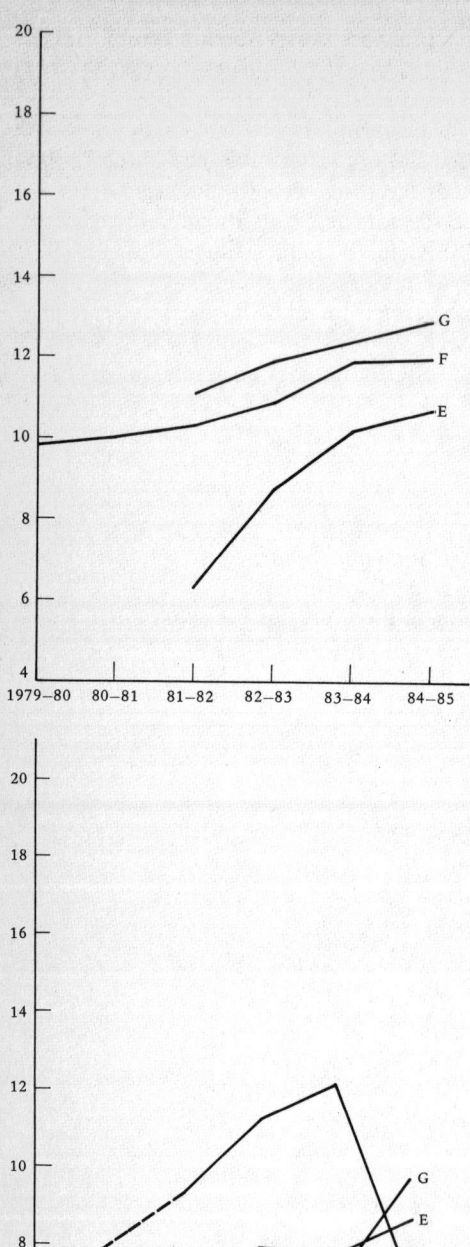

Figure 6.5   SSRs Colleges Group 2
(Poolable)

Figure 6.6   SSRs Colleges Art and
Design (Poolable)

individual institutions grew varied considerably. Polytechnic A, for example, saw only modest growth from just under 6000 students to about 6600 by 1984–5. Polytechnics B and C, however, had increased their numbers considerably. The picture for the colleges in our sample is complicated by the history of merger for three of them and gaps in the data. They had grown, however, though for two (E and F) enrolments in 1984–5 showed a tendency to consolidation rather than continued expansion.

The polytechnics had relatively little non-poolable work, though what they had in three institutions increased slightly, while at Polytechnic D student numbers on non-poolable courses declined. In the colleges, non-poolable courses constituted a greater proportion of their work than in polytechnics, except at College H. In the others, non-poolable enrolments had remained roughly constant averaging around 600.

Staff numbers

While student numbers on the whole had increased in our case study institutions, the same cannot generally be said of staff numbers. For two polytechnics, staff numbers attributable to poolable work had declined – at Polytechnic A by over 200 since the capping of the Pool. The other two polytechnics had increased staff numbers, Polytechnic C in particular. For the colleges, the pattern also varied. There were not dramatic changes in staff attributed to poolable work, though numbers had declined for example at College F but increased at College G. Most colleges had seen a decline in the staff attributed to non-poolable work.

SSRs and the NAB exercise

The institution facing most difficulty in meeting the NAB targets for 1984–5 was Polytechnic A. For a high-cost, low-SSR institution like Polytechnic A, the exercise meant drastic steps to bring spending and SSRs close to the norm. Its SSRs were low because the expansion of student numbers envisaged in its original development plans had not taken place. In 1982–3, its SSRs were 8.6 for Group 1 and 10.3 for Group 2 faculties (for poolable work), a long way short of the 12:1 NAB overall target – though improved from 1979–80. Even so, its proposals suggested an overall SSR of less than 9:1. A similar though milder problem faced Polytechnic D. Despite its elaborate prioritization exercise and proposal to reduce student numbers in line with resources in its response to NAB, it found that its allocated student numbers for 1984–5 required moving to an SSR of 11.4:1, though it actually achieved a reduction in SSR in Group 2 faculties from 14.7 in 1983–4 to 12.9 in 1984–5. It planned that an overall SSR of 12:1 could be achieved by 1986–7, but because increases in student numbers could not be guaranteed, this could only be by reductions in staffing.

Institutions with lower costs and higher SSRs faced fewer difficulties. Polytechnic B could point out that it had 'one of the highest SSRs in the country so academic staff expenditure is below average'. Its initial response to the proposed 10 per cent cut in resources was to reduce student numbers slightly, though this strategy was later reversed. The Polytechnic's NAB response showed an overall SSR of 11.7:1 in 1982 rising to 11.9 by 1983, and in 1985, the Academic Board adopted a policy to achieve a 12:1 SSR.

Polytechnic C had consciously and explicitly anticipated the need for efficiency. During the academic year 1980–1 its Directorate had adopted a policy, known as 'turning up the burner', of pushing up student numbers without significantly increasing staff, to achieve marked increases in SSRs, and lower unit costs, and it was, in fact, able to allow very slight relaxations of SSRs in 1984–5 in both faculty groups. More than one member of the Directorate had experience in government or serving on government bodies and felt in close touch with national thinking. They anticipated that resources would follow student numbers and therefore that the Polytechnic should maintain or increase its recruitment. Student numbers, which had grown from about 2000 in 1975–6 to 3200 by 1979–80, increased further to over 5000 by 1984–5.

College F, too, with its long history of financial constraint was already operating at relatively high SSRs by 1982. They had risen from 8.5:1 in 1976–7 to 10:1 in 1980–1, encouraged by the setting of SSR targets for the College by the local authority. The College's response to the NAB exercise implied, if a 10 per cent cut in resources had been applied, a further increase in SSRs to 13:1 for AFE work and 11.8:1 for the College overall. In the event, for Group 1 work its SSRs leapt from 10.4 to 14.7 from 1983–4 to 1984–5, though there was a drop for Art and Design work from 12.1 to 9.0.

The two 'hybrid' colleges had been operating within SSR bands for some years under the DES direct grant funding arrangements. None the less, the NAB exercise meant a further tightening of these ratios. In January 1984, for example, College E adopted an overall SSR of 10:1 (though a 12:1 SSR for teaching purposes) and concern at the implications of a 12:1 figure was expressed. Nevertheless, an overall target of 12:1 was adopted in November 1984. At College H, the NAB return implied an SSR which exceeded the NAB sector target, at nearly 13:1. It adopted target SSRs for courses according to NAB programme areas of 13:1 and 15:1 for 1984–5 and in its actual allocation of staffing to courses achieved figures as high as 18.3:1, though in Group 1 work there was a small actual decline in SSR from 1983–4 to 1984–5.

For most institutions the preferred method of increasing SSRs was to continue their previous policies of increasing student recruitment in preference to compulsory staff reduction. Institutions were reluctant to force staff reductions and were often prevented from proposing compulsory redundancy by the policies of their maintaining authorities.

Thus, the institutions which had maintained growth policies for some years, such as College F and Polytechnic C, continued them, and the majority of our case study institutions put forward proposals to NAB for increased student numbers, and most, in the event, received targets that gave them this; indeed, several institutions received targets well in excess of their proposals (e.g. Polytechnics C and D and College F). Polytechnic D, which had proposed a

1300 reduction in FTEs ultimately received a target of nearly 1500 in excess of their proposal!

A policy of increased recruitment could be combined with relative ease with one to control staff numbers, by accepting voluntary severance, premature retirement or non-filling of vacancies. Indeed, given a sufficient increase in student numbers, staff growth is possible. Thus the policy of 'turning up the burner' at Polytechnic C by rapid growth of student numbers was allied, as we saw earlier, to some expansion of staff numbers up to 1981 and with the use of PRC schemes, even enabled a 'new blood' policy of staff recruitment to take place.

Polytechnic A, however, faced problems of such magnitude that increasing student numbers could not offer anything like a significant improvement in SSRs. It was forced to shed large numbers of staff not only to improve SSRs but also to reduce costs. The Director's medium-term strategy of October 1982 showed how the Polytechnic's academic staff costs exceeded the mean for polytechnics by 23 per cent, and this was reinforced by the NAB 1984–5 allocation, which meant an estimated 13 per cent (£2.4 m) reduction in real terms. His plans concentrated on a proposal to lose 115 teaching staff by 31 August 1984. This figure derived from an analysis of the Polytechnic's SSRs and the NAB/HMI best-practice figures department by department. Even so, the figure of 115 staff was only just over half that required to bring SSRs up to the best-practice levels. In the event, substantial progress towards the 115 target was achieved, which meant that on top of an historic decline in staff numbers, there was a 25 per cent reduction since 1979.

Similarly, at College E, some 100 out of over 400 staff in its constituent colleges were expected to have left by voluntary means by the end of 1984–5 and a further 8 losses were planned for 1985–6 to achieve stability and a 12:1 SSR. College F had also in the past been obliged to enforce compulsory redundancy on a small number of staff, though this arose when a course was closed on academic grounds.

Centralization of control

The achievement of greater efficiency was generally seen in our institutions as necessitating increased control over resource allocation and utilization. As the Director of one College recognized, 'the 1980s are not times for putting financial control in second place'. While the need for such control was recognized in all our case study institutions, the mechanisms used to attain it varied. Most institutions saw its achievement through increased centralization, involving not only a greater focus on directorates and the relevant academic board committees in the decision-making process, but also increased scrutiny of budgets and spending. Several institutions began to emply zero-based budgeting for at least parts of their spending.

Centralization was not, however, the universal pattern. Within the overall frame of increased scrutiny and control, one institution developed a system of devolved responsibility to cost centres, though the extent of devolution was more limited than it had originally envisaged, and another was beginning to consider devolution.

The major controls developed in our case study institutions were those affecting the allocation and monitoring of staffing. It was through these mechanisms that policies to improve efficiency in terms of increased SSRs were implemented. Institutions with longer standing policies to improve SSRs had generally already developed such systems by the time of the NAB exercise. Others found it necessary to tighten their procedures or develop new ones. Only one institution found it necessary to introduce a special review process. College F, for example, already had a policy of centralization of staff allocation at the time of the NAB exercise derived from the lessons it learnt from its past. Its allocation process involved an annual cycle with heads of schools submitting returns of current figures and bids for the coming year to the Deputy Director, who made the allocations after considering the resources available. The allocation was based on and monitored by an elaborate 'triangulation' system using data from three sources – a staffing schedule for courses from heads of schools, individual staff timetables and a return of allocations of staff to courses by the subject divisions. At the time of the NAB exercise this process was undertaken manually, though it has been transferred to the FEMIS microcomputer system.

A similar complex central control system had also been developed at Polytechnic C as a necessary part of its strategy of 'turning up the burner'. The post of Special Assistant to the Director was created with the task of developing an information system for monitoring SSRs, so that the Directorate policy of establishing minimum SSR levels for courses could be implemented. The Staff Schedules Analysis system (SSA) is based on individual termly staff timetables, verified by the head of department and processed by the Special Assistant to the Director, and it produces SSR figures and FTE allocations at various levels, such as department, subject area or individual lecturer.

The need to meet new and tighter SSR levels as a result of the NAB exercise led, at College H, to the development of a new system for staff deployment. Controls already existed over overall SSRs, though there was no precise control over staff time. Since its inception in 1977, the College had operated at a 12:1 ratio for all programmes: it now had to move again, to 15:1 for BA programmes for example. The new policy involved agreeing SSRs for each programme area, then a series of 'programme profiles' for each course in terms of lectures, seminars, tutorials, etc. to check that total teaching hours were within total allocated staff hours. Staff allocations were made by the Deputy Director in conjunction with the programme and section heads and the staff concerned. So tight was the control that for the 1984–5 allocations, the SSR targets were exceeded for several programmes, though this was mainly caused by unexpected departures of staff.

Polytechnic D was the only institution to employ a special procedure to determine SSRs in the wake of the NAB exercise. Here it was recognized that the achievement of a 12:1 SSR which was significantly higher than that previously planned by the Polytechnic was not going to be easy and the special review procedure was established by the Academic Board to establish a set of department guide SSRs compatible with the overall target and taking into account other changing circumstances. This review was carried out by the Deputy Director visiting each department accompanied by the Dean and two staff members from the relevant Academic Board Committee, though it was made clear that this review was not intended to do the jobs of, or undermine the existing structures of, resource allocation.

In deciding which SSR levels to aim for institutions had basically two choices. They could accept the NAB/HMI 'best-practice' SSRs on which their NAB allocation had been based, or they could devise their own internal targets. Our institutions were split, with the majority opting for the NAB figures, though in some cases modifying these slightly. History, again, played some part in this decision. Institutions – such as College F and Polytechnic C – with established allocation and control systems tended to have their own targets already and were not inclined to modify them radically. Indeed, at College F, the NAB/HMI figures were rejected out of hand by the Director, and actual SSRs have a much wider range than the best-practice figures. At Polytechnic C the NAB figures were rejected because they did not take account of the institution's heavy emphasis on research. Both these institutions were already close to NAB SSR levels anyway. For institutions which had to implement greater change in a short period of time it was generally easier to import outside guidelines than to develop their own *ab initio*.

All our other institutions, however, applied the NAB/HMI figures to their various courses as part of their staff deployment procedures. NAB/HMI figures were (with some local variations) also used as a basis for calculating staff numbers and the need for potential staff losses. This happened dramatically at Polytechnic A, when the Director put forward proposals for accommodating the anticipated shortfall for 1984–5 of more than £1.5 m. These contained an analysis department by department of actual and target SSRs based on the NAB figures and suggested an ultimate loss of over 220 staff.

Increased control was also exercised by our institutions over other aspects of their spending, and new mechanisms were developed to deal with these items too. Institutions scrutinized all their budget heads to see which could be reduced. No items were sacrosanct and no saving too small, though most institutions sought to protect areas where cuts would lead to unacceptable standards. College H, for example, reported in its return to NAB that it had been through a period of systematic reappraisal of its main areas of expenditure, and as well as reducing academic staffing costs, it had undertaken establishment reviews of non-academic staffing and restructured its support services; it had contracted out its catering and residence, and withdrawn new course proposals. It made a series of small savings on such items as telephone bills, staff travel and charging students for materials, though it had protected spending on staff development and the library. Polytechnic A undertook an examination of all its budget heads, so that all non-staff spending was 'pared to the bone' by 1984–5. Polytechnic D, anticipating continuing cuts in budgets after suffering from the initial 'capping' of the AFE Pool contained spending on part-time and visiting staff, froze vacancies, encouraged staff to take unpaid study leave and generate income through consultancy, strictly controlled procurement and expenditure on heating, lighting, telephones and printing. Polytechnic A undertook a substantial review of its non-academic staffing and reduced its establishment, prior to the planning exercise, by over 150 posts.

To maintain control on these items, however, resource allocation procedures were tightened. It was on non-staff items that departments had traditionally had most freedom. In most of our institutions budgets were based on historical figures and directorates and staff in several institutions accepted that they had not been subject to great scrutiny. With constraint, this began to change, and moves toward 'zero-based' budgeting began to appear. Thus College F saw the need for increased central control by its schools over spending as one of the main lessons of its history of constraint. The College introduced what is basically a zero-based budget system for the allocation of resources to schools, which are required to justify their budgets in detail, instead of receiving an allocation based on the previous year's budget. Individual capital items over £1000 also require individual justification. This lesson is allied with another based on the experience of the past, which is the need for a large contingency within the budget. About 20–30 per cent of the schools' budgets are withheld centrally and an initial allocation made only for the first 7 months of the year. When student enrolment begins in October, the College Directorate negotiates with schools on allocations to reflect developments. Even then a small reserve is withheld. The ability to shift resources is thus seen by the Director as a key feature enhancing the institution's ability to respond to constraint, though the schools have only marginal control over their budgets.

A similar approach was also developed at College E for its allocation of resources to faculties for equipment and materials and staff development. In 1984–5 a new system was introduced, replacing a system of bids from the faculties and cost centres to the Deputy Director who then prepared summary papers for the appropriate committee of the Academic Board. The new system is a two-stage one, with bids prepared in a format suitable for copying to the Committee which attempts to identify an allocation sufficient for each area to function at a minimum but acceptable level. The allocation of remaining money is then considered from a zero-based budget view to meet needs, agreed developments and to support priority areas.

At Polytechnic C, levels of non-staff resources are determined by the Directorate consistent with its management style and policy of 'turning up the burner', based on FTEs and modified NAB weightings. The process is highly centralized and decisions are described as simply 'handed down' to the faculties. Although individual Deans may negotiate with the Deputy Director (Resources) the margin for change is generally tiny. Faculties do, however, have considerable freedom to distribute their allocations to departments, and the Polytechnic is considering moving to a cost-centre system.

Revision of their arrangements for charging and costing short courses and other entrepreneurial activities was also found necessary in some institutions.

Polytechnic A discovered when it introduced budget-centred accounting that there were considerable discrepancies in the way in which faculties handled short courses. The lack of clear management policy on the aims of short courses and on ways of treating their finances led to a major review by the management accountant. His new system of accounting for them started from the proposition that it was no longer possible to cover only marginal costs; surpluses could be generated only when income exceeded the total of all costs including properly apportioned overheads. Polytechnic C had also found difficulty in establishing a clear policy for short course accounting. It had made a distinction between programme short courses which generated FTEs and *ad hoc* courses which were full cost with the department retaining any surplus income. Most departments sought to classify all their courses in the second category and a review was generally thought necessary of the whole system. Both these institutions had also sought ways of coping with some of the problems of local authority regulations on income generation by establishing companies to handle consultancy and other income-generating activities.

While all of our institutions responded to the need to control expenditure by increasing central stringency, some also attempted to combine this with devolved responsibility for control to cost centres. The major development along these lines was at Polytechnic A, though other institutions such as College E treat faculties and other units to some extent as cost centres. In none of our institutions could a true cost-centre system be said to be in operation, as the freedom to generate and spend income is heavily constrained. The crucial issue is of course staffing: if full control is to be offered, then this head must be included in devolved responsibility; if it is, then overall control to move to target SSRs may be lost. No institution has, so far, gone to this level of devolution. Thus at Polytechnic A, the Director's original aim in introducing the budget-centre system was to get individual departments to examine their spending and income-generating activities. Under the previous system resources were allocated to the faculties where the Dean had the power to decide how to distribute money and allocate staff between departments, at least in theory. The Polytechnic's overall spending was handled only in terms of heads of expenditure, and continued reductions in resources meant that cutting heads had a differential impact on departments depending on their level of spending. By dividing up the whole Polytechnic into budget centres and giving each centre a spending limit for the financial year, this system would give departments more control over their own spending and an incentive to generate their own income. This original plan, however, was not implemented in that form because the Directorate felt it took too much control away from them during the course of the financial year. The management accountant designed the new system somewhere between the Director's original plan of yearly budgets and the plans outlined in the CIPFA guide, which divides the institution into cost centres, teaching and non-teaching, and then looks at methods of describing all income in terms of teaching centres. The objectives of the new system were to stimulate resource competition and upward financial control (supply better information to the Directorate and Governors on relative spending of departments) and allow individual budget holders more control over spending. In its implementation, the last objective of giving greater freedom to budget holders had dissipated. A further similar problem arose at another institution (Polytechnic C) where the attempt to allocate central costs to cost centres proved complex and controversial.

Restructuring

In order to improve their efficiency several institutions felt it necessary to not only adopt policies to increase SSRs and control spending but also to change their structures. The most extensive restructuring occurred at Polytechnic A, as part of its new Director's medium-term strategy of late 1982. When the Polytechnic had been formed, the three original colleges were brought together on a faculty basis, with considerable overlapping. The next stage was to have the faculties more autonomous, with control over their resources. Deans of the faculties also became Assistant Directors with responsibility for Polytechnic-wide functions. At the peak, there were 10 Assistant Directors, including 8 Deans, but even before the appointment of a new Director, the previous Director had reduced the number of faculties from 8 to 6.

The medium-term strategy's restructuring of academic departments involved a reduction of the number of faculties to five, intended to produce 'more coherent groupings of departments' as well as managerial and financial benefits by reducing the number of units and (in the longer term) expenditure on senior staff salaries. Later, in 1984, the Polytechnic was restructured again, abolishing the faculties, whose functions had become unclear, in favour of a structure based on departments which interrelated through boards of studies.

There was restructuring in some of our other case study institutions, though less extensive than at Polytechnic A, and in some cases not directly related to constraint, as we discuss on page 74. However, the relationship between the faculties and the Academic Board at College E was reviewed after a CNAA visit, reflecting a 'need for effective and efficient communication throughout the College'. Polytechnic B embarked on consideration of restructuring its faculties and Academic Board Committees, a move which was seen as facilitating prioritization in the future, though its ostensible purpose was to improve academic planning.

Relocation

Restructuring was often associated with the relocation of parts of institutions in an attempt to reduce premises costs, inter-site travel and other costs of a multi-site operation. Here again, institutions' responses – and needs to respond – depended to a considerable extent on their previous history, particularly if they had been formed from mergers. Nearly all our institutions had been created in this way and had more than one site. Again, Polytechnic A was involved in the most extensive changes. A study here attributed costs totalling approximately £1 m to its multi-site operation in 1984–5. The Polytechnic had withdrawn from its site in one of its constituent authorities in summer 1983, but its medium-term strategy involved efforts to relate faculties and departments to location and further relocation of staff and departments. Efforts were made to reduce the number of buildings in use, though this could not always be achieved because of the reluctance of the local authority to take back responsibility for the building or for legal reasons with leased property. The Polytechnic also attempted to seek more support from an adjoining authority for its jointly run management centre, and terminated its agreement with the authority, a tactic which resulted not in a new more favourable agreement but the acceptance of the termination by the authority and the loss for the Polytechnic of the management centre premises in the authority.

At Polytechnic B, the main concern was an isolated building, formerly a college of education but now part of the Polytechnic, which it wished to vacate but would be unable to do so until 1987. Relocation of most activities from this site was planned for 1986, to improve effectiveness, space utilization and reduce split-site operation. A similar historic problem faced College E. It had five sites in 1983 with high maintenance and repair costs, and problems of duplication of resources and subjects taught. Detailed consideration of alternatives took place, but it was not until 1985 that agreement was reached on consolidation on four sites, involving the relocation of several departments.

6.2 Academic planning and structure

As we saw in our discussion of institutional strategy in Chapter 5, institutions rarely plan their activities on the basis of formal 'mission statements'. Strategies are more commonly related to underlying assumptions about the character of the institution and what Davies and Morgan (1982) call its 'core values'. At the same time, academic policies are often developed by Directorates, despite the formal responsibilities of various bodies, particularly Academic Boards and their committees, for academic planning. While Directorates may play the crucial role in developing academic policies, however, they need to build consensus support for them within the institution, which means that these bodies still have a crucial role to play.

In examining the range of structures and procedures for academic planning in our case study institutions, several important issues emerge. The first concerns the locus of decision-making and whether we can identify changes related to financial constraint. The second issue concerns the impact of different faculty/departmental structures on decision-making and implementation of policy. Third is the coordination between resource and academic planning and the fourth involves the assessment of quality and the importance of procedures for monitoring and evaluation of courses.

The locus of decision-making varied in our case study institutions with the size, composition and structure of the bodies charged with formal responsibility

for academic planning. According to most instruments and articles of government, the Academic Board is formally responsible for the planning, coordination, development and oversight of academic work. The Director or Principal is
normally charged with the management of the institution. This distribution of
responsibility raises two issues. There is a basic contradiction between the role
of the Academic Board as a representative body and its role as policy-maker;
and there is the question of the execution of policy and the need for quick
decision making. If the Academic Board is to provide a forum for discussion of
issues allowing representation from all the various sectors of the institution, its
size would preclude the kind of quick action required of a decision-making body.
Academic Boards thus rarely play a decision-making role.

This problem is usually recognized with the formation of smaller committees
given the power to recommend action which is then formally adopted or rejected
by the Academic Board as a whole. As Shattock and Rigby point out, however,
smaller committees can be seen as unrepresentative and so small that full
discussion with a wide range of views expressed does not occur:

> Against this it must be said that large and seemingly democratic commit-
> tees can sometimes, particularly under strong chairmanship, behave
> almost like rubber stamping bodies in which complex and sensitive issues
> and possible alternative courses of action are seldom discussed
> seriously. . . . Nevertheless, even if a large committee normally behaves
> like rubber stamp, the knowledge that the awkward question may be
> asked and the rubber stamp withheld can still have a powerful influence
> on the formulation of policy. (Shattock and Rigby 1983, p. 59)

Shattock and Rigby give the example of one university which reduced the size
of its Senate in order to make it a more effective decision-making body, but this
arrangement involved an unusually small proportion of staff and actually had
the effect of reinforcing the power of the Vice-Chancellor, Pro Vice-Chancellors
and Deans over the elected members (ibid., p. 60). A similar example could be
drawn from Polytechnic C, which has a relatively small Academic Board with
only three major committees. The planning of strategic policy is limited to only
a small number of senior staff who have been described as a 'kitchen cabinet'
meeting on an informal basis. The Academic Board committees are seen by
the Director as deliberative rather than consultative and it is generally acknowledged that the Academic Board tends to rubber stamp decisions taken
elsewhere. This structure is congruent with the 'executive' style of the
Directorate and its tendency to control decision making.

It has been argued that financial constraint requires the kind of quick action
and flexibility that can only be embodied in small decision-making bodies and
executive freedom of action. A look at all of our case studies does not, however,
point to a trend toward smaller academic boards and committees or toward
more executive power. In the case of Polytechnic C the Director had always
been known for his executive style and the Academic Board had not been
involved in decision making during the years of economic growth. In fact, this
structure of academic planning proved to have its drawbacks in a period of

financial constraint, revealed by the resentment felt by staff at each level below the Academic Board that executive decisions could not be challenged on academic grounds. Heads of departments who had no representation on the Academic Board felt shut off from policy discussion, but members of the Board themselves felt that it could not even act as a forum for discussion because of lack of information from the Directorate. The Directorate's decision to prioritize as part of the NAB exercise had the effect of opening up discussion of institutional strategy and making more information available at lower levels for the first time.

In contrast, College F had been characterized by a very participative structure of academic planning before the impact of financial constraint. When a decision by the Academic Board to close a department on academic grounds led to staff being made compulsorily redundant by the local authority, the reaction of staff members was to withdraw from consideration of decisions involving cuts in funding. As a result, the Academic Board opted out of consultations on the College's response to the NAB exercise, giving the Director a free hand. This policy had been questioned by some staff even before the College's financial position improved as a result of NAB's final allocation, and the Academic Board has tried to take a more active role in decisions on how to spend the extra funds. While these developments could be characterized as a move toward more executive action, they seem more a temporary reaction to the crisis caused by cuts in funding and were initiated within the Academic Board and the teaching union rather than as an attempt by the Directorate to play a more powerful role. In fact, the Directorate is aware of the drawbacks of not carrying staff with them in decisions on the future shape of the institution and it seems unlikely that the participative tradition in the college has been permanently abandoned by the Academic Board.

The temporary adoption of special procedures or the use of *ad hoc* working parties is characteristic of a crisis response and several examples of such practice can be found in our case study institutions. Polytechnic D tended to make use of special working parties with governing body participation to tackle particular issues. The ranking of courses as part of the NAB prioritization exercise was carried by one such *ad hoc* group and another working party was charged with developing a staffing strategy. The drawbacks of such a procedure were seen by Shattock and Rigby (1983), who point out that while such small groups may be able to take quick executive action, their decisions are unlikely to generate consensus, particularly where clear criteria for evaluation have not been agreed. Evidence from Polytechnic D supports this contention, since the prioritization exercise caused particular controversy and is still remembered with resentment.

It seems from the evidence of our case study institutions that academic boards should play a more positive role by discussing medium- and long-term goals for the institution and providing a forum for discussion of general policies. Of course, the size of cuts and the urgency of the crisis is a factor which cannot be ignored. Polytechnic A faced a major loss of funds in one year with little prospect for improvement in subsequent years. The Academic Board is large and traditionally played a political role, providing the arena for various power groupings to operate. The role of its committees was much less clear and attempts to reorganize and clarify their functions ran up against the size of cut facing the Polytechnic and the need for major changes in a short time. The opportunity for consultation was limited by the urgency of the crisis and the Directorate clearly played the decision-making role in developing policies to meet the shortfall. On the other hand, the Director was aware of the importance of building consensus and was able to mobilize staff on the basis of resistance to outside threats to the institution's survival.

The academic board and its committees do not provide the only forum for academic planning, since considerable responsibility for decisions about courses and investment is embodied in departments/faculties depending on the academic structure of the institution. The lack of any clear trend toward smaller academic boards or more powerful committees is also reflected in the lack of any identifiable trend toward greater centralization in faculty/departmental structures. In fact, the only clear trend in this area is toward change, in whatever direction. The effort being put into restructuring in our case study institutions, however, cannot be attributed only, or even primarily, to financial constraint. One characteristic of restructuring is that such policies can accomplish a number of different objectives, which means there are often hidden agendas on the part of directorates, who are normally the initiators of such policies. While restructuring is normally justified on academic grounds, the other objectives range from the desire to get rid of unsatisfactory buildings or sites to the elimination (or formation) of higher-level academic posts. The usefulness of restructuring policies for a newly appointed director to make his mark within the institution may mean that such policies will be favoured whatever the other objectives involved.

Our case study institutions provide ample illustrations of all these objectives, particularly since a number of them had newly appointed directors in the period of our research and mergers were also a major factor in some cases. Two examples demonstrate not only the presence of hidden agendas, but that such restructuring did not tend to move in a particular direction.

Polytechnic B moved to a stronger faculty structure after the appointment of a new Director. The new structure gives more responsibility and administrative support to the bigger faculty units rather than the departments and the loose aggregation of departments into faculties has been modified in some cases with a matrix structure. Problems with sites as a result of mergers were also clearly important factors. In contrast, Polytechnic A went in the opposite direction under its new Director, eliminating faculties and the high-level posts of Dean and giving more responsibility to departments both as cost centres and in academic planning. This structure was described to the CNAA as a way of combining strong central direction with bottom-up participation through the departments.

One unintended consequence of the usefulness of restructuring for a wide range of objectives is that the restructuring may itself come to dominate the institution. Polytechnic A, with its large number of sites and departments, for example, has a tradition of continued restructuring which has had the effect of undermining stability and lowering morale among academic staff. With all the uncertainties in a time of financial constraint and the short time frame available to academic planners because of outside constraints, the additional disruption caused by internal restructuring can add substantially to their problems.

In general, directorates prefer the kind of line management structure embodied in department/faculty systems, while teaching staff concerned with participation in academic planning prefer matrix structures. The advantages of a matrix structure were seen at College F in terms of a greater role for teaching staff who could influence course development and staff allocation through 31 subject divisions. This matrix structure co-existed with a powerful Directorate which tightly controlled deployment of staff and resource allocation. A major conflict arose within this institution, however, over the roles of senior academic staff. Some teaching staff wanted heads of subject divisions to be seen as academic leaders and opposed the desire of the Director to bring in highly qualified outsiders to newly created senior positions. This controversy demonstrates a more general problem of all academic structures: the conflict between administrative, teaching and research roles for deans, heads of departments, schools, divisions, etc. To the extent that senior academic staff are seen as line managers and given considerable administrative duties, it is less likely that they will play a crucial role in research and/or teaching or be seen as leaders in their academic fields.

The problem of administrative versus academic roles for senior academic staff leads into the third issue to be examined concerning the relationship between academic and financial planning. If it were possible to clearly distinguish between resource allocation and academic planning it might be sensible to make all financial planning the responsibility of the directorate and administrative support staff and leave academic staff with course planning and educational policy-making. This distinction is very difficult to make in practice, however, and the impact of financial constraint has been to introduce more financial criteria into academic planning. A good example of this kind of problem can be seen in Polytechnic C where the Directorate's decision to increase student numbers without increasing staff meant a considerable rise in SSRs. This strategy was seen as a way of ensuring favourable funding for the polytechnic on the basis of its low unit costs. This kind of 'efficiency' policy, however, was imposed by the Directorate as part of its management of financial costs and the possible academic consequences were never debated by the Academic Board. The powerful Planning Committee, which combined responsibility for both academic and resource planning, required that all new or revalidated courses attain a minimum SSR. Some staff criticized this policy as part of a planning process which was narrowly based on statistics and financial priorities and failed to allow discussion of the trade-offs involved in 'efficiency' policies.

Most of our other case studies separated responsibility for financial and academic planning in separate academic board committees, but while this might provide a better forum for discussion, it does not solve the problem of whether decisions will be finance-led and whether institutions will take account of the price they pay for taking 'efficiency' options. There was a clear trend in our case study institutions for academic planning to take account of resource issues in a much more open way. In general, the procedures for review of current courses and approval of new courses have been modified to include consideration of their resource implications. Polytechnic A's criteria for course reviews now include student intake and SSR projections as well as the effect on facilities and support services. College E reorganized its planning procedures and faculties are now expected to draw up their own plans for courses, considering their resource implications. The Academic Board also undertook a course review which includes consideration of resource availability as part of the process.

The importance of resource considerations can also be traced in a more active role for resource committees (or their equivalent), but while they may discuss policy on the resource implications of course development, it is not always clear whether resource or academic considerations will have the highest priority. Where strong directorates insist on the use of standard indicators like SSRs, they may dominate resource committees and restrict planning to statistics on student numbers and staffing levels. The coordination of resource allocation and academic planning depends to some extent on the relative membership of resource and academic committees and on their relationships to the directorate, but the lines of responsibility are not usually firmly drawn.

One problem for academic planning committees is the difficulty of quantifying academic values. While it is not difficult to establish SSR levels it is difficult to show, for example, that the value of a certain course justifies a higher than average investment in resources and staff time. The Jarratt Report (CVCP 1985) has recommended the use of performance indicators in academic planning but has failed to define these indicators or suggest how they might be developed. Many institutions have identified a large number of criteria for course evaluation, but have found it difficult to agree which criteria should have the highest priority and many criteria involve value judgements without an established way of measuring performance. College E developed a set of nine criteria and was considering the development of specific output measures, such as pass and attrition rates, to evaluate courses.

Beyond the issue of the quality of courses is their importance to the local or regional community or the level of student demand. Where an institution has established traditions of excellence in particular areas or particular courses which serve the local community or industry, it may be easier to assign priorities. Polytechnic A is committed to providing access to local students, which requires an emphasis on part-time modes and innovative course structures, such as independent study. Despite the crisis caused by serious cuts in funding, the Directorate did not reject these commitments, while acknowledging the unfavourable resourcing available for some of this work. This kind of problem also faced College H, where one of the three major areas of work which provides a service to the local community involves school-based in-service teacher education and consultation. This area was threatened under NAB funding because it no longer generates sufficient FTEs and income for the College and it is still unclear whether the priority given to this type of work will survive the effect of new funding formulae and financial constraints.

Still, even where priorities are given to areas which are threatened by unfavourable resourcing, at least these institutions have reasonably clear objectives which could provide the basis for the discussion of priorities in academic planning. Where objectives are unclear, the difficulty of quantifying academic values and establishing priorities means that committees with responsibility for academic planning often make decisions without reference to any generally accepted principles on long-term goals and, as we saw earlier, there are few examples in our case study institutions of the kind of strategic planning envisaged by the Jarratt Report (CVCP 1985) or other writers such as Sizer (1982) and Davies and Morgan (1982). Market research into possible areas of high demand or programme reviews require considerable lead time and investment, as well as clear lines of authority. The exact responsibilities for academic and financial planning are not clearly defined in most of the academic structures in our case study institutions, although recent restructuring plans are expected to address this problem. *Ad hoc* responses to financial constraint, however, can leave academic boards and their committees open to control from directorates. The increasing importance attached to financial considerations may push academic planning in particular directions which are not necessarily congruent with the institution's character and traditions.

Along with an increasing emphasis on financial considerations, there is a trend in our case study institutions for academic planning increasingly to emphasize quality and the importance of evaluation and monitoring of courses. Nearly all our case study institutions felt the need to tighten up monitoring and evaluation of courses and procedures for approving new courses. Many moved to an annual course review cycle with standardized course reports and they have tried to establish clearer criteria for evaluation. This reorganization usually also involved changes in the composition and responsibility of the committee in charge of this function.

Some of the procedural changes in course monitoring can be related to the institutions' changing relationship with CNAA. Many of the polytechnics have moved beyond validation of new courses, having obtained long-term approval for many courses requiring only a periodic progress review. CNAA's request for proposals for new forms of 'partnership in validation' led Polytechnic B, for example, to propose that they move to self-validation, while retaining links with CNAA. Polytechnic B felt the review of previously approved courses required modifications in course monitoring procedures giving more responsibility to departments and course committees. Annual reporting on course reviews was also introduced at Colleges E, F and H.

While these changes in procedures can be seen as a response to CNAA or other outside bodies, they also reflected increasing financial constraint. With cuts in funding threatening, pressures to prioritize inevitably led institutions to consider how courses were evaluated and try to defend their academic profile by reference to its quality. The definition of quality, however, can vary widely between and within institutions. The desire for self-validation also involved aspirations for status, which were found in many of the colleges and poly-technics in our sample. Faced with the prospect of reductions in funding, it is not surprising that institutions began to look with longing at higher-status institu-tions which they saw as better resourced. The directors of a number of our case study institutions found that aspirations for university or polytechnic status could mobilize staff in support of their policies, but such aspirations could also have some unintended consequences in terms of issues like the quality of courses.

For example, Polytechnic B's desire to move to self-validation led to an increasing emphasis on quality, defined at least to some extent in terms of 'centres of excellence'. The concept of centres of excellence came up in other case study institutions, such as Polytechnic C, which aspired to university status. Where certain subject areas are considered sources of particular strength, it is not surprising that institutions emphasize them as centres of excellence, but when combined with an aspiration for higher status, the identification of quality with centres of excellence may lead to a priority on higher-level courses or research at the expense of what some see as the traditional role of public sector institutions. Polytechnic B found that their commitment to part-time and sub-degree work was threatened by such a priority. Emphasis on research, postgraduate programmes and publications may be consistent with the definition of quality in terms of centres of excellence and encouraged by CNAA, but it may mean that the quality in teaching and reward for the development of innovative course structures or teaching methods is less valued.

Polytechnic C's efficiency strategy meant higher SSRs and some teaching staff felt there was less time available for course development or research. When combined with aspirations for university status, which led to an emphasis on research and postgraduate work, some staff complained that teaching and course development came a poor third. This complaint was shared by some staff at College F, who pointed out that it was easier to quantify research in terms of the number of publications, while important work on the development of new teaching materials went unrecognized. College E also aspired to polytechnic status, which created an impetus to develop masters' programmes and an increased emphasis on the improvement of quality of provision. In contrast, College H did not aspire to higher status and traditionally saw its strength in terms of student-centred teaching. The major change in its academic structure was the introduction of 'packaging' of courses which was seen as improving both efficiency and academic quality. In this case, however, quality was defined in terms of increasing the range of choice available to students and increasing the range of experience of teaching staff in a small institution.

6.3   Implications

The policies adopted by our case study institutions on resource allocation and academic planning and structure have a number of implications. As we saw in the discussion of institutional strategies, there was a general lack of long-term planning and formal discussion of specific strategic objectives. While this may have given more freedom to directorates to take executive action, we also saw that it could mean that institutional strategies did not generate consensus. But there are further educational implications of this kind of response. Crisis responses to financial constraint may generate policies whose implications are never fully examined by the responsible planning bodies. As a result, institutions may not be aware of the unintended consequences of their responses to financial constraint.

Some of these unintended consequences become clear when we examine the implications of our institutions' responses to the imperative to improve efficiency of the NAB planning exercise. Changes in SSRs, for example, have had effects on the nature and structure of courses, the workload of staff and the demands placed on the facilities and accommodation of institutions. The consequences of these developments have, in turn, raised questions about the meaning of efficiency for some of our institutions. The pattern of response has also raised concerns about the capacity of institutions to respond to these kinds of imperatives and the different interpretations they made of the likely nature of the NAB exercise.

One of the now familiar formulae in institutions is the relationship used to calculate Pooling Committee SSRs:

$$SSR = \frac{ACS \times ALH}{ASH}$$

where ACS = average class size, ALH = average lecturer teaching hours and ASH = average student taught hours. For the Pooling Committee's purposes, this formula is superior to the straightforward division of FTE students by FTE staff because it incorporates information on the deployment of resources and the effects of different teaching patterns. Changes in SSRs clearly involve changes in one or more of these variables.

Institutions' returns to the Pooling Committee's monitoring survey, which we analysed earlier in this chapter to identify changes in SSRs since the AFE Pool was capped, also include data on these SSR factors. These data show that for the polytechnics in our sample, increased SSRs for poolable courses over this period have mainly been achieved by increases in average class size (ACS) (see Figures 6.7 to 6.9). All four polytechnics show increases in this measure, with Polytechnic A again the most dramatic; its class sizes in art and design, for example, rose from 6.4 to over 14.

While class sizes have increased in our polytechnics, the amount of time spent by staff teaching them has remained remarkably constant (reflecting conditions of service agreements which have not generally changed over the period). Only at Polytechnics A and B is there a slight indication of an increase over the period (Figures 6.10 to 6.12).

The abbreviations used in the following Figures are explained below for clarity.

ALH   Average Lecturer Hours – The total curricular hours of all lecturers for each level of work are first divided by the number of weeks and then by the total number of FTE lecturers to give ALH.

ASH   Average Student Hours – The total curricular hours of the full-time students (for the whole academic period only) are divided by the number of weeks and then by the number of students to give ASH.

ACS   Average Class Size – Multiply the number of full-time equivalent students by the ASH and divide by the total weekly curricular hours of all lecturers.

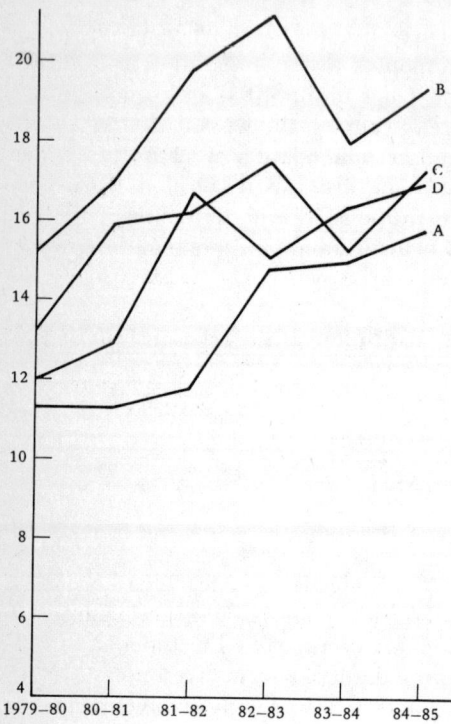

Figure 6.7   ACS Polytechnics Group 1 (Poolable)

The pattern of change in average student hours (ASH) is more difficult to identify and interpret (Figures 6.13 to 6.15). One clear feature is that our polytechnics in 1984–5 were less disparate in this respect than they were in 1979–80. In some earlier years there were very wide variations between institutions. There also appears to have been a trend for average student hours to increase in the first few years after the Pool was capped but then to decline so that figures for 1984–5 were close to the average for 1979–80.

Overall, of our group of polytechnics, the most interesting is perhaps Polytechnic A, in which the most rapid increases in SSRs have been achieved mainly by the high level of teaching hours but which is offset by longer class hours (high ASH), so that it still has lower SSRs than the other polytechnics in our sample.

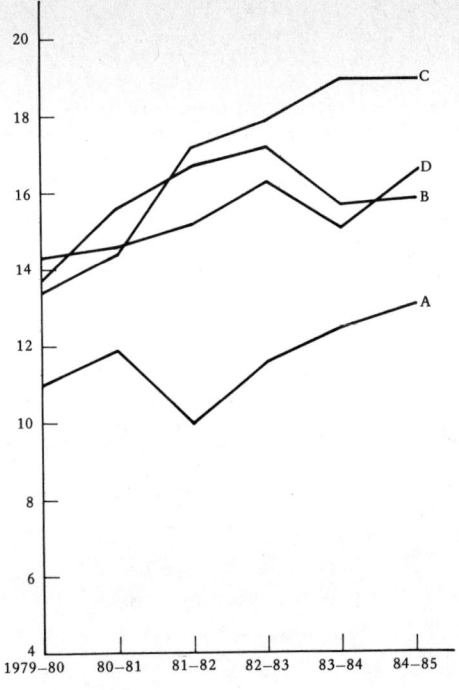

Figure 6.8 ACS Polytechnics
Group 2 (Poolable)

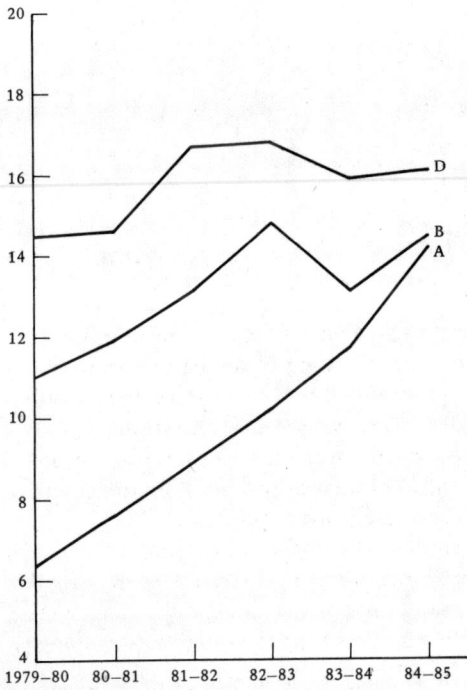

Figure 6.9 ACS Polytechnics Art
and Design (Poolable)

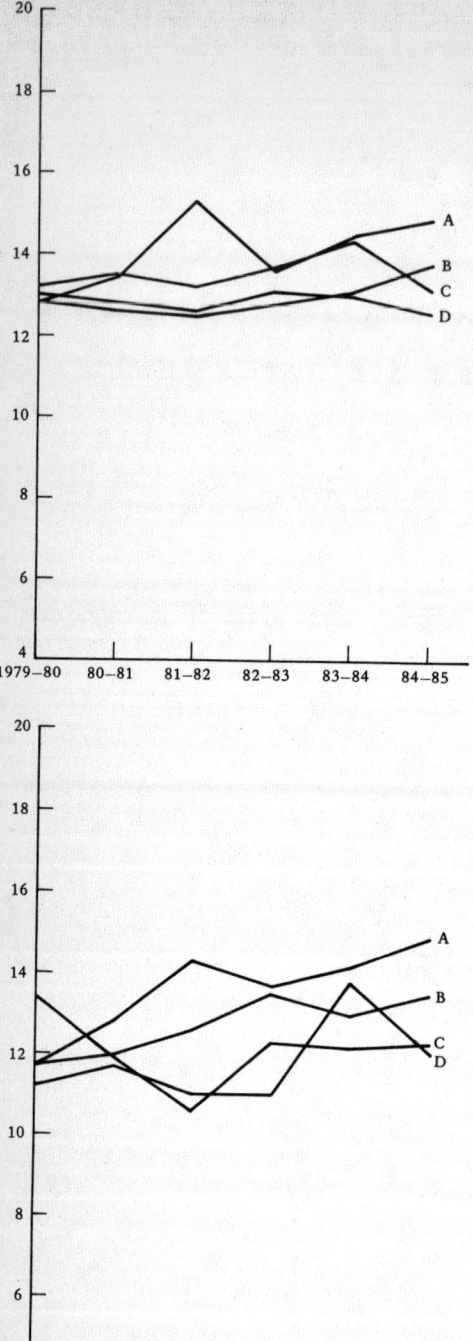

Figure 6.10   ALH Polytechnics
Group 1 (Poolable)

Figure 6.11   ALH Polytechnics
Group 2 (Poolable)

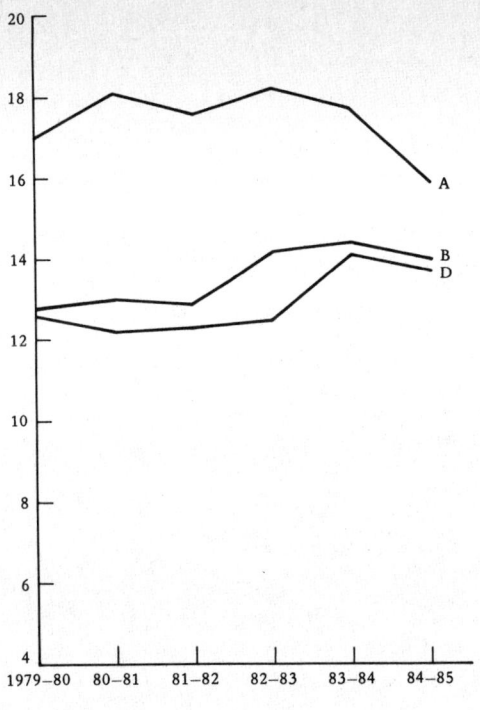

Figure 6.12 ALH Polytechnics
Art and Design (Poolable)

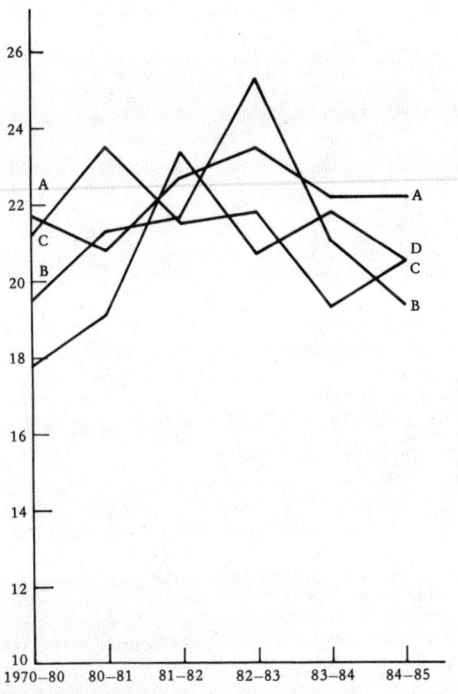

Figure 6.13 ASH Polytechnics
Group I (Poolable)

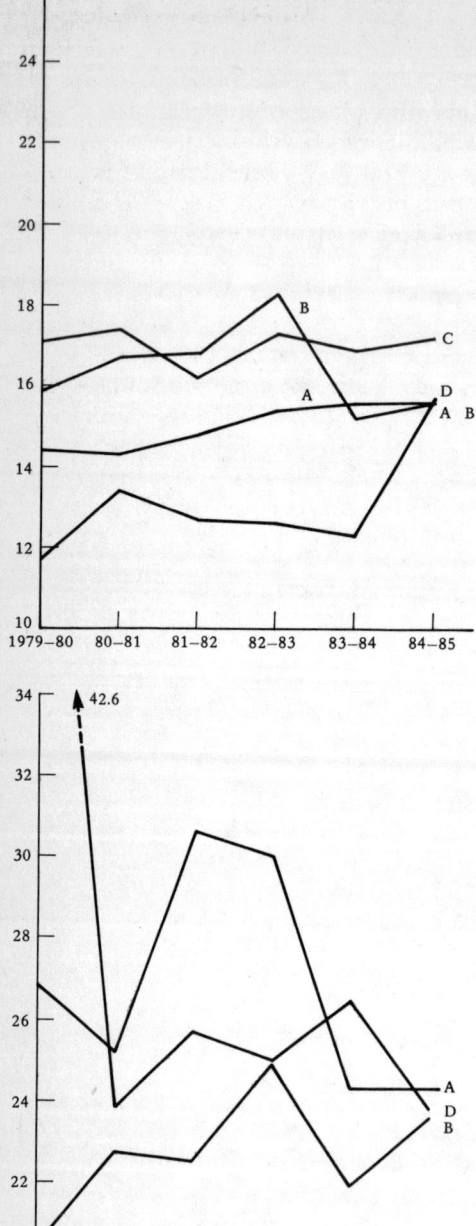

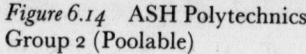

Figure 6.14   ASH Polytechnics Group 2 (Poolable)

Figure 6.15   ASH Polytechnics Art and Design (Poolable)

In our colleges the limitations of data and greater variety in changes in SSR mean that the changes in these three variables are more disparate and offer a less clear pattern than in the polytechnics. There is some indication that average class sizes for poolable work have coalesced (see Figures 6.16 to 6.18) and in the case of College F generally increased, but other colleges show declines on several occasions. Average lecturer hours like those in polytechnics remain generally consistent (Figures 6.19 to 6.21), though College F again shows an increase. Average student hours give a clearer picture (Figures 6.22 to 6.24): these have mostly decreased, often from remarkably high levels and the colleges now teach students for similar, shorter periods each week.

It is clear that higher SSRs imply a more widespread use of large teaching groups. To increase average class size most of our institutions are increasing overall enrolments to courses and modules (subject to and sometimes in defiance of NAB targets). College F had a policy for some time of accepting very high SSRs in areas which could in the Directorate's view cope with them, while also 'going after' schools and courses with low SSRs, and selectively excising poor recruiting courses. Polytechnic C's policy of 'turning up the burner' meant increased recruitment and larger group sizes, and it benefits in recruiting students from what is called the 'Bath syndrome' (an attractive location for students).

Institutions are also recognizing that SSRs can be increased by reducing the number of hours spent in contact with teaching staff (ASH). College F, for

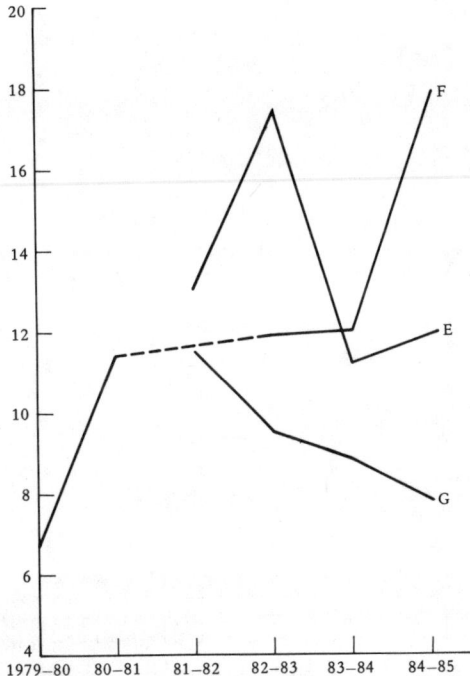

Figure 6.16   ACS Colleges Group
1 (Poolable)

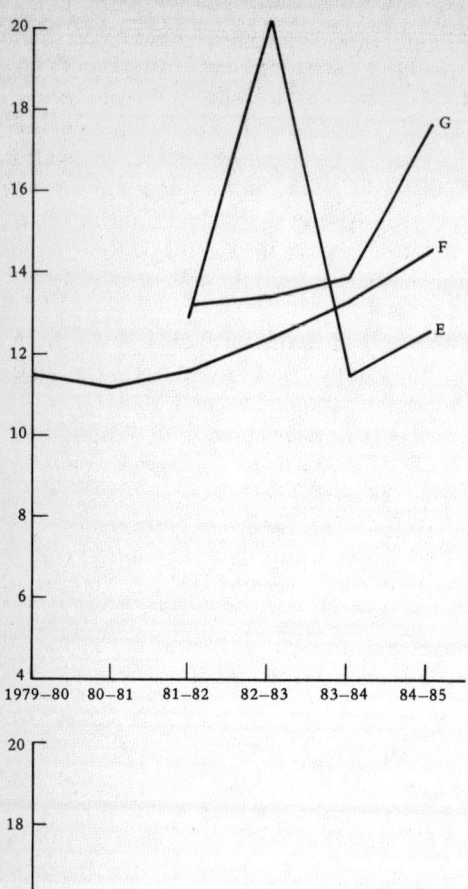

Figure 6.17   ACS Colleges Group 2 (Poolable)

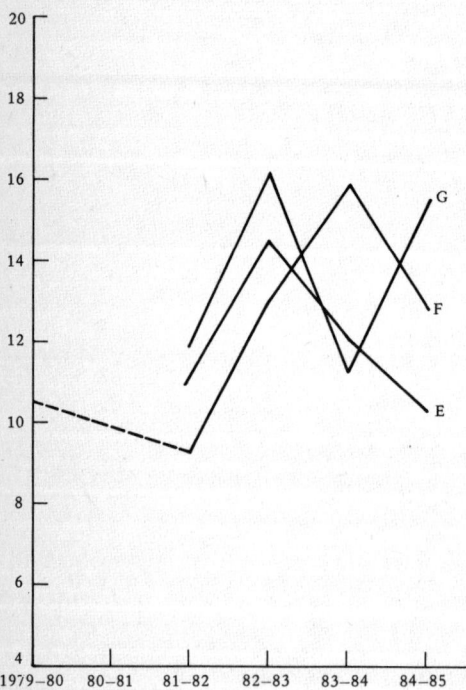

Figure 6.18   ACS Colleges Art and Design (Poolable)

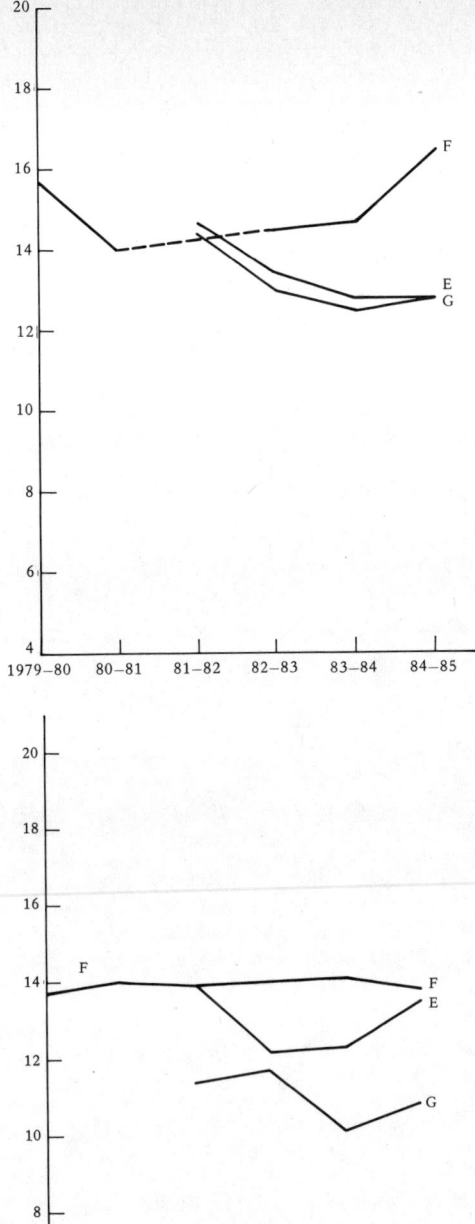

Figure 6.19   ALH Colleges Group 1 (Poolable)

Figure 6.20   ALH Colleges Group 2 (Poolable)

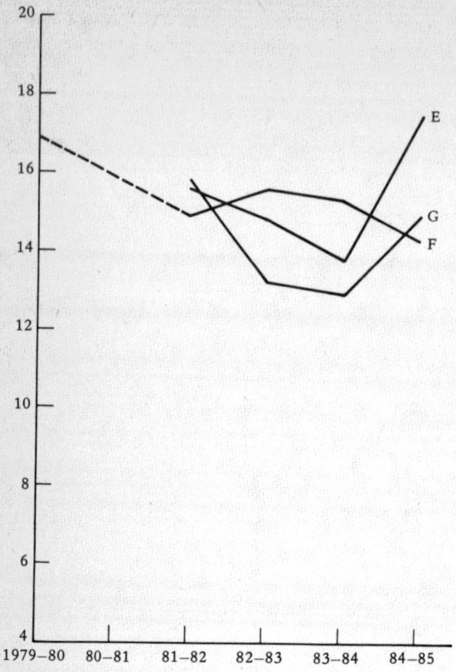

Figure 6.21   ALH Colleges Art and Design (Poolable)

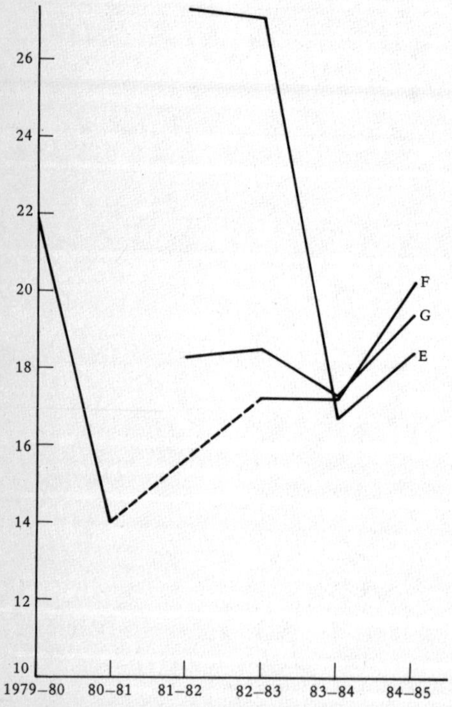

Figure 6.22   ASH Colleges Group I (Poolable)

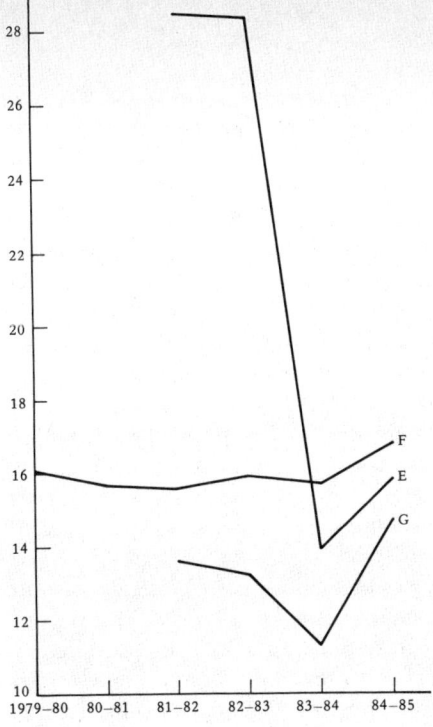

Figure 6.23   ASH Colleges Group
2 (Poolable)

Figure 6.24   ASH Colleges Art and
Design (Poolable)

example, is attempting to reduce its traditionally high contact hours (more than 20 per week in 1979–80) in recognition both of the need for improved SSRs and of the overteaching that these figures imply. At Polytechnic C, the Planning Committee explicitly agreed a policy of low average lecturer hours (12 hours per week) in return for higher class sizes as well as fewer remissions against class contact time.

The moves towards higher SSRs have implications not just in terms of class sizes and student and staff hours, but also in terms of the structure and nature of courses and teaching. Several of our institutions were examining their course profiles and teaching requirements to accommodate higher SSRs, though at others this was still at an early stage. Polytechnic A, for example, stressed to the CNAA in 1984 that it placed 'great importance on the development of new teaching and learning methods and on staff development as part of its academic plans to adjust to the new staffing situation', and reported the formation of a new information and resource centre based on the library to support these developments. On the other hand, at College E, an increase in innovatory activity was felt to be 'more talk than action'; a minority of staff, however, recognized that new teaching methods and combining teaching on some courses would need to be introduced.

Changes in average group sizes and contact hours have generally meant changes in teaching methods. The main change is from individual tutorials or seminar discussion towards formal lectures. Staff at several institutions reported that this was having adverse effects on the quality of teaching. In part this kind of problem arises because it is rarely possible to increase group sizes *pro rata* with SSR increases. There are usually reasons for retaining small groups on some courses or parts of courses. This means that small groups must be compensated for elsewhere on the course or in the institution. At College F, for example, staff reported that tutorial groups may have ten or more students, so that it becomes no longer possible to describe it as a tutorial. Institutions are devising a variety of teaching patterns to cope with these problems. Institutions are seeking to combine lecture classes where possible, so releasing staff time and resources for smaller group work. At College F, one course has an introductory programme with groups of 70 students.

There is thus some indication that group sizes and teaching methods are polarizing. Instead of working for most of their course in groups of around the average SSR figures, students are taught for some of the time in large groups and for the rest in small ones. A version of this polarization occurs in College H which employs different group sizes according to the stage of the course. For some of its courses students work in small groups at the beginning of the course when high staff inputs are felt to be needed while the students establish themselves, and in the last year when they are working in specialist areas of interest, for example on a project. The intervening period makes more extensive use of lectures with large groups.

Other responses involve changes in overall course structures. Several of our institutions were revising their courses along modular lines to maximize resource curtailments, combining teaching of similar students on different courses or, as at College H, to 'package' courses in related studies, or to maximize NAB weightings. However, one consequence of this is thought to be the reductions of options available. Whilst the course itself may continue, the range of choice within it may be reduced, because staff are heavily timetabled and cannot make their expertise available, or because staff with relevant experience have been lost. At Polytechnic C options are reported to be reduced because servicing departments are reluctant to continue to supply staff because their own courses are already using them.

There is a less obvious but potentially more sinister aspect of loss of range of content. Whilst most institutions are still able to continue offering courses some have reported that the range of material that can be presented to students on courses is reduced, mainly because staff resources or teaching hours have been reduced. Thus, it was said, students on a history programme who might have been introduced to four or five different approaches to history now do not get that range of material presented or presented to the same extent.

Similar fears were expressed about loss of quality in several areas where small group teaching is regarded as essential. At Polytechnic C courses with a high practical content require 'hands-on' experience with expensive equipment which can only be taught in small groups. Some staff pointed out that it was precisely the practical aspects of these courses which made their students attractive to employers. The possibilities for field work and project work were also felt to be threatened by higher SSRs, with 'paper' exercises sometimes replacing actual field work, despite its importance to many engineering and science courses. Similar problems were reported with in-service education courses at College H, which required visits to schools to acquire actual teaching experience. Such requirements meant additional travel expenses as well as small groups. At Polytechnic A, clinical experience required as part of training for psychology courses also required small groups and expensive laboratories.

Changes in average student taught hours (ASH) relate, of course, to average lecturer teaching hours (ALH). An increase in SSRs can be achieved by increasing the ALH. Institutions, as we saw earlier, are introducing more stringent control of lecturers' timetables in order to ensure that they work at or near (and sometimes in excess of) agreed contact hour maxima. Despite evidence of the Audit Commission that in further education as a whole there is evidence that teaching staff are not working to the levels implied in their contracts, staff in several of our institutions reported that increased SSRs meant increased teaching hours and increased administrative burdens, which prevented their undertaking important other tasks related to the quality of course provision such as research and course development. It was mainly in institutions with explicit policies to achieve high SSRs that these problems were voiced, particularly College F and Polytechnic C, but also at Polytechnic A where rapid increases in SSRs were attained in a short period by staff reductions. At College F one of the problems pointed out was that much of the increased workload is not recognized in contact hour measures. Higher SSRs increase marking and administration time even though staff hours may remain the same: a kind of 'iceberg effect'. At Polytechnic A, concern was widely expressed that the Polytechnic's ability to develop new courses and maintain its innovative tradition would be hampered by increased pressure on teachers, and the sudden loss of staff as well as repeated restructuring caused discontinuities in courses and uncertainties for staff.

Increasing pressure on staff from higher SSRs at Polytechnic C was seen as cutting into the time available for research and course development. Some staff here also complained of the 'iceberg effect', i.e. a heavy marking load and less contact with students. In an institution with a heavy emphasis on research, the preparation of course materials was felt to have suffered, despite the benefits of developing new teaching methods and materials.

The pressure to increase SSRs had implications in some of our institutions for their accommodation. This arises in two ways. Responses which involved large or rapid increases in student numbers placed demands on the total space available to the institutions. College F, for example, has operated with a space deficit for many years, and repeated accommodation surveys showed shortfalls up to 4000 square metres against DES Design Note standards, and CNAA had recorded in 1980 for example that staff accommodation was 'simply inappropriate for staff engaged in higher education'. While this resulted principally from growth in recruitment outstripping space made available by the local authority, the second difficulty arises from changes in teaching group sizes.

Some institutions found that their room sizes were inappropriate for the teaching groups they were now obliged to use. At College F this meant a reversal of policy. In earlier years, rooms were partitioned to create seminar spaces and accommodate small classes. Some of these have now had to be reconverted to accommodate the larger classes necessitated by increased SSRs! At Polytechnic C, staff reported a shortage of laboratory space, though overall the institution has benefited from a building and renovation programme. The major problem here, and at College F and some other institutions, is a shortage of student residential facilities, again problems exacerbated by increased recruitment.

Similar consequences of policies and procedures to improve efficiency arose for support services and other facilities of institutions. As we saw earlier, while institutions sought to preserve certain areas from the effect of cuts, policies to make savings in non-academic staffing resulted in considerable problems in some institutions. College F had been criticized by CNAA in successive quinquennial visits for the inadequacy of its technical and support staffing and had to switch scarce resources into these areas. Because it had been poorly funded in the past, its eventual increased NAB allocation for 1984–5 enabled it to redress some of these deficiencies. In another institution (Polytechnic C) the LEA has taken an active part in controlling numbers and grades of non-academic staff and the Polytechnic feels it is understaffed, particularly while trying to cope with increased numbers of students.

In the areas which were protected, constraint has also had its effects. Libraries are the main case in point. Book funds are particularly vulnerable to inflation and most institutions can show that real purchasing power has been reduced substantially. Staffing in libraries has been described by one Head of

Learning Resources as 'critically low' (Polytechnic C). Another (multi-site) institution has considered plans to reduce the number of its libraries and to reduce hours of opening.

The implications which we have discussed in this section have not necessarily been addressed by the appropriate planning bodies of our case study institutions. The pressure of outside constraints and the increasing importance attached to resource considerations in academic planning have not been counterbalanced by efforts to evaluate the impact of efficiency policies. The difficulty of quantifying academic quality and the tendency to define it in terms of 'centres of excellence' have also added to the task facing those responsible for academic planning. Changes in teaching methods and the development of innovative course structures to counteract the problems identified in this section will not be developed unless these implications are addressed and priorities are established between resource and academic considerations.

References

Committee of Vice Chancellors and Principals (CVCP) (1985) *Report of the Steering Committee for Efficiency Studies in Universities*. CVCP.

Davies, J. L. and Morgan, A. W. (1982) The Politics of Institutional Change. In Wagner, L. (ed.) *Agenda for Institutional Change in Higher Education*. Guildford: SRHE.

Shattock, M. and Rigby, G. (eds) (1983) *Resource Allocation in British Universities*. Guildford: SRHE.

Sizer, J. (1982) Assessing Institutional Performance and Progress. In Wagner, L. (ed.) *Agenda for Institutional Change in Higher Education*. Guildford: SRHE.

7

The Constraints of the Public Sector

John Pratt and Michael Locke

The behaviour of institutions cannot be explained solely on the basis of the individuals within them, as Popper has pointed out (1962, p. 90). Whilst individuals and their motives, and indeed the motives of groups, are part of any explanation, these must be supplemented by an analysis of the environment in which they operate. For institutions of higher education this environment is complex and changing; for institutions in the public sector it is particularly complicated, with formal controls placed upon them from both local and national government, and pressures from a range of other parties at both levels. In this chapter we examine one of the major factors that influenced institutional managers in their responses to constraint and the NAB planning exercise – their relationship with their local authorities. This relationship differed between the two kinds of institution in our case study. The maintained colleges and polytechnics belong formally to the authority, and the NAB return, for example, had to be submitted to the authority. The hybrid colleges as, legally, voluntary colleges were in a partnership with their authorities. Not surprisingly the experiences of the two kinds of institutions differed, but there were also marked differences in the relationships within the group of maintained institutions.

The problem of the relationship between institutions and their authorities has received considerable attention over a number of years. The key issue was encapsulated in the Weaver Report (1966, para. 10):

> the problem was to strike the correct balance between the freedom which institutions of higher education should enjoy and the social control which democratically elected representative bodies are required to exercise.

The Weaver Committee was established to find a solution in terms of institutional governance, and the present arrangements of institutional governance which we outlined in Chapter 2 derive from their report.

7.1 Institutional governance

The Weaver solution was to define the responsibilities of the authority (or providing body), the governing body and the academic board and principal.

The Committee started from the conviction that 'the affairs of a college are primarily for academic people to deal with' and so recommended that every college should have an academic board which, subject to the general approval of governors, would be responsible for its academic work (para. 11). Local authorities were in the last resort responsible for the college, its efficiency, financing, staffing and premises, and for its size and character. The governing body should be responsible for the general running of a college and its broad pattern of courses.

When the policy to designate polytechnics was initiated, DES Administrative Memorandum 8/67 required local authorities to draw up instruments and articles of government along the lines described by Weaver, as a precondition of designation. Similar provisions were made for voluntary colleges under the Training of Teacher Regulations 1967. This was followed by the Education (No. 2) Act 1968, requiring similar articles and instruments to be produced for other colleges and 2 years later by DES Circular 7/70 which advised on the implementation of the 1968 Act. It was under these provisions and guidance that the articles and instruments of our case study institutions were made and, later, revised.

Despite these provisions it is not unfair to say that the central problem of striking the balance between institutional freedom and control by elected bodies has not found a generally satisfactory solution. Locke (1974) observed for example that many of the recommendations contained in both Administrative Memorandum 8/67 and Circular 7/70 were regarded with great suspicion by the LEAs. The crucial problems revolve around the extent to which local authorities should intervene in the detailed management of their institutions. The Weaver Committee had recommended giving considerable financial powers to the governing body. It would be responsible for the approval or amendment of estimates of expenditure and the academic priorities they implied as expressed by the academic board. However, because responsibility for expenditure ultimately lay with the LEA it was emphasized that all transactions should be in accordance with the financial regulations of the LEA, although it was hoped that these would not be overly restrictive. The difficulty inherent in the proper control of expenditure through detailed annual estimates and the need to make efficient use of funds was also acknowledged, but a greater measure of *virement* was proposed in order to cope with changing needs and priorities; and special funds were proposed whereby money could effectively be carried forward from one year to another in respect of those areas of expenditure such as repairs, maintenance and equipment which vary from one year to another in the level of spending required. The use of LEA services for repairs and maintenance, for example, should be required only where it could be shown to be financially advantageous.

Within the confines of approved estimates the governing body should be free to determine academic staffing levels and grading, though it was acknowledged that the LEA should exert influence over the number of non-teaching staff posts in order to maintain broad comparability between the various institutions it maintained.

Despite the requirements of Administrative Memorandum 8/67 and Circular 7/70, an enquiry established under the chairmanship of Gordon Oakes, Minister of State for Education and Science, observed in 1977 that there was still

> a wide variety in the way in which institutions are in fact managed, and it is a common complaint . . . that some local authorities intervene in the detailed management of their institutions so as effectively to prevent governing bodies from exercising the responsibilities for management entrusted to them by their institutions' articles of government. (Oakes 1978, para. 8.2)

The question of the freedom of operation of institutional managers was raised again when a House of Commons Select Committee investigated the funding and organization of courses in higher education (1980). In presenting evidence to the Select Committee the Committee of Directors of Polytechnics (CDP) argued that the polytechnics should be removed from the control of the LEAs and placed instead under the control of a national body. The opposing arguments were presented by the local authority associations, but the question was apparently settled by a submission from the Secretary of State which came down on the side of the LEAs and a continuation of the *status quo*. However, the Select Committee said that:

> we believe that it will only be acceptable for local authorities to retain their stake in higher education if all of them can restrain themselves from excessive and unreasonable interference in the running of large developed polytechnics with the skills and competence to look after themselves. At the very least, duplication of bureaucracy is unacceptable. (Education Science and Arts Committee 1980, para. 72)

None the less, the LEA associations continued to argue in a review group on college government established during 1980 by the Council for Local Education Authorities (CLEA) that the composition of some articles, including the model articles contained in Circular 7/70, impeded LEAs in the exercise of their statutory, financial and employment obligations, which had changed and increased in scope during the 1970s (CLEA 1981). The LEAs argued that it would be necessary for them to be able to alter financial estimates during the course of the financial year, have greater control over staffing establishments, the power to redeploy staff both within and between institutions, a reserve power to dismiss staff without the support of the governors, increased control of courses and power to close existing courses and launch new ones. A corollary of this would be a reduction in the powers of academic boards and that overall responsibility for college management should be withdrawn from the Governing Body and that the governors be made accountable to the LEA.

It is against this background of the radically conflicting views of institutions and authorities of their relationship that we begin our examination of the way in which this relationship affected their responses to constraint. We look first at the formal distribution of powers and responsibilities in instruments and articles of government.

7.2 Instruments and articles

The instruments and articles of government of our two groups of institutions (maintained and 'hybrid'), while defining their system of governance, differ because of the different legal status of the institutions. The six maintained institutions (four polytechnics and two colleges) of our case studies are not legal entities in themselves; the local authority is legally responsible for them. The two 'hybrid' institutions have been established by trust deeds and are legal entities and have charitable status. Their trustees are ultimately responsible for them, and the trust deeds appoint representatives of the Church of England and the county council. For the maintained institutions the instrument and articles of government regulate the relationship between the institution and the LEA. For the voluntary colleges the instrument and articles set them between the LEA, Church of England and Secretary of State for Education and Science (because of his responsibility for the direct grant funding of voluntary colleges).

Instruments and articles of government follow the model established in Circular 7/70, but no two sets of instruments and articles of government are identical (other than for some colleges in the same authority). Many of the differences are minor, often without readily apparent practical consequences. But some differences are potentially larger in their impact: the clarity with which the powers of LEA and governing body are specified; the size of LEA representation on the governing body; the allocation of financial responsibilities; the decision-making powers of the academic board; and some include particular items of significance. The tendency established through debates and policies about college government during the past 40 years is for colleges undertaking more advanced work to have powers more extensively devolved to and within the college.

The compositions of the governing bodies for the eight case study institutions are fairly typical. Governing bodies usually consist of 36 or so members, though three of the case studies have more than 40 (Polytechnic B, Colleges E and G). Within this total the LEA has substantial but not majority representation, commonly about one-third or less; but as well as the question of numbers there are variations as to whether the LEA nominees are specified as elected members of the authority or its education committee or whether the LEA can appoint or nominate from outside its own ranks. The largest local authority representation among the case studies is that in College F, where 12 out of a total body of 36 are 'from the Authority or its Education Committee', and in Polytechnic A 12 out of 39 are 'elected members' of the three constituent authorities. The smallest LEA representation is in Polytechnic C where seven are 'appointed' by the LEA in a body of 38 and in Polytechnic B where seven are 'representing' the authority in a body of 46. In most cases neighbouring authorities or, variously, county councils or city councils are also represented: a further two nominees in College F and Polytechnic A, three in Polytechnic C (plus the Lord High Steward) and seven in Polytechnic B.

In the two hybrid institutions the governing bodies are founded on seven representatives each from the Church of England and the LEA, though in College E the County Council then has three appointments in addition to its seven 'foundation governors'. All case study governing bodies include representatives of academic staff from both the academic board and from elections, non-academic staff and students. All include the director/principal; College H and Polytechnic C include two and one deputies respectively.

A third major component of governing bodies is that of persons having 'appropriate' or 'relevant' experience of industry, commerce and the professions: 5 at College H and 8 at Polytechnic A, but in others 10–12. Sometimes included within that component, but more usually a separate group, are people with experience of working in education or nominated by universities and other educational institutions. College H is unusual in having an open-ended clause for nominees from the academic bodies validating its qualifications.

The articles of government establish the functions of the four main components in college government. The LEA is typically described as having the power to 'determine the general education character of the college and its place in the local educational system'. The governing body is given the 'general direction of the conduct and curriculum'. The director/principal is responsible for the 'internal organization, management and discipline', and the academic board for the 'planning, coordination, development and oversight' of academic work. The case study institutions in some cases further clarify the powers or specify the functions. Polytechnic D, under the general descriptions for the LEA and for the governing body, lists 15 functions for each of them; among those which rest with the LEA are 'to determine the broad range of courses to be provided . . . and to approve an academic development plan, after considering any recommendations of the Board of Governors' and 'in consultation with the Board of Governors to review the general organization and management structure . . . to review its efficiency and to advise the Board of Governors thereon'. These clauses indicate the LEA's concern for its responsibilities over, first, the range of courses and, secondly, the management of the polytechnic. Determining the 'broad range of courses' is also included in Polytechnic B's statement of the LEA's functions. College F goes further in that the LEA 'after consulting with the Governing Body . . . , shall decide: (a) the principal areas and general nature of the academic work which shall include the approval of new courses; (b) the location and size of the college; (c) the financial resources to be made available'. Polytechnic A notes the financial powers reserved to the authority. Polytechnic D in its list of functions includes one to cover safety legislation. It also includes the LEA's power to determine 'within any limits specified by the Secretary of State for Education and Science, the size of the Polytechnic'. Polytechnics B and C also recognize the impact of national policies.

Prima facie there is a constitutional difference between the statement of the LEA's responsibility for the range of courses or approval of new courses and the more relaxed statement in Polytechnic C: 'in consultation with the Governors and where necessary with the Secretary of State for Education and Science, for determining the general educational character'. Of the two hybrids, College E ascribes the 'educational character' to its governing body, while College H does not make such a general statement.

Most of the case study institutions use only the broad 'general direction' statement with respect to the function of the governing body. Polytechnic D and College F, as with their LEA statements, push for greater clarification and pinning down of responsibilities. College F reasserts the LEA's concern over academic expansion: 'make recommendations to the Authority for the establishment of any new course and provide the Authority with the necessary information relating to resource implications and estimated student numbers'. College F also requires the governing body to monitor the aims and work of the College and report to the LEA.

The functions of the director/principal also mostly follow the conventions, though here too Polytechnic D specifies functions in more detail. Polytechnic A adds a phrase about the director's responsibility for the 'deployment of resources'. The two hybrids lay a responsibility for the Christian aspect of the college at the directors' feet. Polytechnic D is unusual in writing into the articles of government two committees of the governing body: an Education Programme Committee to keep under review the 'objectives and balance' of the education programme and to consider academic proposals in conjunction with the academic board and governing body; and a Resource Committee to 'prepare and keep under review a plan for the resource needs', to prepare annual estimates and exercise powers over expenditure.

The formal role of the academic board as established in articles of government normally follows the model of Circular 7/70 of the 'planning, coordination, development and oversight' of academic work. Six of the case study institutions have a general statement which uses this wording, and two follow its spirit but with different phraseology. Polytechnic D refers to 'policy, balance and development' and College G to 'oversight and regular review of all academic work' and 'promotion, planning, coordination and development of both new and existing courses'. Articles of government then normally set out more detailed functions covering responsibility for the examination and assessment of students, admission and exclusion (on academic grounds) of students, research and consultancy, and often consultations with the governing body on arrangements for the appointment of staff, the preparation of estimates or resource planning and allocation of academic staff within the establishment.

In broad terms the case study institutions follow this pattern, though they differ much in the way these functions are set out. Some of the variations appear not to be of much practical impact: the difference between making 'suitable arrangements' and 'regulation' for the admission of students, for example, might not amount to much in practice. Polytechnic B and College H include statements about the academic board's responsibility for teaching practice, though it seems unlikely that other academic boards would be considered not to have this responsibility if their institution is involved in initial teacher training. However, there are potentially more significant variations over the academic board's involvement in resource issues. Only Polytechnic C among these institutions has articles of government which give no role to the academic board in resource matters, though Polytechnic D only provides for the academic board's involvement in resource proposals as part of an academic development plan. By contrast, the articles for College F have the academic board 'reporting on the resource implications of proposals to vary or extend the work of the College', making recommendations to the governing body on the allocation of staff and consulting with the director on the internal allocation of resources. College G includes advising the director on the allocation of funds, on teaching and non-teaching staff establishments and on the annual estimates. Polytechnic A has 'recommendations about allocation of resources including staff', and Polytechnic B 'consideration of and recommendation on' estimates. Colleges E and H have the academic board consulted in the preparation of estimates and being involved in decision-making about the allocation of academic staff within the establishment.

A crucial aspect of the relationship between colleges and their local education authority is the financial relationship established by the articles of government. The pattern of the current system is that the governing body submits annual estimates of revenue expenditure to the LEA and that, when these have been approved, the governing body is authorized to spend in accordance with those estimates but remains constrained in a few major respects where it has to defer or refer to the LEA. One constraint is that the college must use, or at least have regard to, the purchasing arrangements which the LEA has made with various suppliers. One can readily see the issues at stake: on the LEAs' side the questions of the efficiency and economy of the system for which they are responsible; on the institutions' side their autonomy and their view that they know best what they need to buy. The common statement in articles of government is like that of Polytechnic C: '. . . to place orders for supplies (including equipment) and services at their discretion subject to their making use of the central purchasing arrangements of the Authority where this would be more economical'. Frequently, a figure is written into this clause which gives the governing body freedom to spend below this amount, and the articles for Polytechnics A and B set a figure of £100 above which the governing body must make use of central purchasing arrangements where 'more economical' (though both these articles were being revised). The other four maintained institutions do not have a figure specified in the articles – in this respect the case studies are not a representative sample as most polytechnics specify a figure. Prima facie it would seem that not having a specified figure implies greater constraint in that all purchasing should make use of the authority's arrangements. However, the nuances of wording might be important. College G gives the governing body more discretion in stating: 'The (governing body) may place orders for supplies (including equipment) and services at their discretion, subject to it making use of the usual purchasing arrangements of the (LEA) where the (governing body) is satisfied that such arrangements would be more advantageous'. Polytechnic D is more limited: '. . . the (governing body) shall use the central purchasing arrangements . . . of the Local Education Authority'.

A parallel constraint is that in carrying out repairs, alterations, maintenance, etc., the governing body often has to consult with the local authority. In many institutions, and in five of the case studies (Polytechnics A, B, C and Colleges F and G) the governing body is given freedom to act on its own discretion below a specified figure, such as £500 (College F), £1500 (Polytechnic C) or £5000 (College G). A typical statement is (Polytechnic A): '. . . to carry out repairs, maintenance and minor alterations up to a figure of £2500 per job (or such larger sum as may be agreed from time to time by the Authority) by what they judge, having regard to economical management, as the best means'. Some institutions (e.g. College G) state that this must be 'after consultation with the County Architect'. A tighter hold is written on Polytechnic D: '. . . the (governing body) shall use . . . the professional and other services of the Local Education Authority'.

Further detailed controls are embodied in financial regulations and standing orders drawn up by the local authority and applied to the college under the powers of the articles of government. These cover such matters as book-keeping and accountancy, procedures for placing orders and purchasing, and conditions for contracting and tendering.

Articles of government also regulate another dimension of the financial government of the institutions. The governing body is authorized to spend within the agreed estimates but an important question is how far in its actual spending decision it is tied to the estimates. Maintained institutions are not given 'lump sum' budgets, but governing bodies are authorized to make their own decision *within* each heading of the estimates, to exercise *virement* within the headings of the estimates. Hence, the number of headings has important consequences for their freedom: fewer, more broadly drawn headings allow more discretion to the governing body. The formal headings available to the case study institutions vary from 7 to 16. One maintained institution – the one with seven headings (College G) – goes further and gives the governing body power to authorize *virement between* headings.

Another important area is the governing body's power relative to the LEA on the establishment of academic and non-academic staff. The basic statement, common to the case study institutions (with only insignificant changes of wording) is 'to determine within the approved estimates the total number and grade of academic staff'. But the nervousness of LEAs is indicated by Polytechnic D's inclusion in its 15 functions of the LEA (see above) 'to issue directions from time to time and particularly to the Board of Governors upon questions relating to the salaries, titles and conditions of service', College F's 'having regard to the . . . conditions of employment and service as adopted by the local education authority' and College G's 'subject to the Council's conditions of service'. Polytechnic B holds back the power over the principal's and deputy principal's salary scale to the LEA.

Additional cautions are introduced on non-teaching staff in some cases. Polytechnic D asserts all questions about salaries, wages and conditions of service 'shall be in accordance with such directions as may be issued from time-to-time by the Local Education Authority to the Board of Governors'. Polytechnic B is similar though adds 'after consultation with the Governors', and College G says that remuneration and grades are to be 'agreed' with the

LEA. Polytechnic C tells the Governors to 'review the numbers and grades of non-academic staff annually prior to submitting recommendations and estimates to the Authority'.

This discussion has shown that the formal constraints under which our case-study institutions operate while they follow an overall similar pattern vary considerably in detail. Some have considerably greater formal freedoms than others. Interestingly, the polytechnics do not generally have greater autonomy than the maintained colleges and, in some specific instances, they have less; the maintained institution with the most financial autonomy was College G. The 'hybrid' colleges generally have most freedom. Their governing bodies are not constrained by a requirement to use LEA services. The 'hybrid' institutions also give their governing bodies more freedom than most maintained institutions, with the power to authorize *virement between* headings, though College H is limited to 10 per cent of a heading or £1000 (whichever is greater). Their governing bodies have the power to determine establishments of teaching and non-teaching staff within approved estimates (and in the case of College H 'any directions issued by the Secretary of State').

We turn now to the way in which these formal relationships operated in practice in our institutions and their effects on responses to financial constraint.

7.3 Financial support

All our institutions received funds from local authorities; the maintained institutions are 100 per cent local authority funded, the two 'hybrid' colleges were 4/9ths and 74 per cent LEA funded. For advanced work in all institutions, funding came via the AFE Pool. The extent to which Pool funds were explicitly made over to the institutions had varied, and prior to the establishment of NAB was simply not known precisely in one of the hybrid colleges. Funding for non-advanced work was in all cases the responsibility of the LEA, and most institutions – often for some time – had received considerable further direct authority support over and above AFE Pool funds for advanced work – a contribution known (somewhat misleadingly) as 'topping up'. The level of support varied widely, however. At Polytechnic A it was as high as £2 m in 1981–2, though in the next year £360 000 was rebated to its LEAs. Here, topping up represented the balance between the Polytechnic's attempts to constrain gross expenditure and a worsening financial environment. In another polytechnic, the authority's commitment included financing a research assistant scheme as part of topping up. Only one institution (College F) was in an authority with a 'no topping up' policy (though it had made good a deficit in the AFE Pool in one year). This institution had historically had a poor relationship with its authority, and had suffered a history of constraint as the authority imposed budget reductions as part of its overall policy for financial stringency, and this had resulted not only in high SSRs (as we discussed in Chapter 6) but also inadequate accommodation and supporting facilities. One of the lessons of this period for the institutions was the need to improve its relations with its

authority. Most authorities were also working towards a reduction or elimination of topping up; one did so from 1984–5, and several had fixed a specific date
by which time this was to be achieved, thus placing further constraints on their
institutions. Even authorities wishing to maintain such support faced their own
problems of finance. Rate Support Grant cuts caused one LEA to propose
reducing its topping up and this led to a heated exchange with Polytechnic C.

Faced with the prospect of constraint in the NAB exercise most institutions
had sought to retain LEA financial support, even though their authorities
themselves faced reductions in resources. In their responses to NAB, institutions stressed the importance of their courses in meeting local needs and their
ties to local communities to support their case for retaining their academic
profile. Several relied on local 'topping up' to tide them over severe cuts. This
even applied to the hybrid colleges, one of which for example placed great
emphasis on the part it played in the authority's provision for AFE as a whole.
In addition to direct financial support, a number of authorities adopt supportive
roles particularly through the technical and professional services which are
made available. A number of authorities effectively subsidize their institutions
through, for example, charging for services on a marginal cost basis or lower, or
by meeting some proportion of rate costs. Even in our hybrid colleges the local
authority connection is regarded as a valuable source of services, advice and
support, though in these cases the colleges are able to obtain services elsewhere
or provide their own.

LEA policies

While institutions could look to their authorities for financial and service
support, they are nevertheless bound by their authorities in important ways,
both in terms of general policy and in procedural detail. As we have seen, an
authority is responsible for the size and character of its institutions. Its overall
financial policy determines its level of financial support, even for the hybrid
colleges. As local authority institutions, maintained colleges are bound by the
policies of their LEAs in other ways. In particular, they may be constrained by
no-redundancy policies. A number of our case study institutions reported that
they were unable to introduce compulsory staff redundancy for this reason,
although in one institution which had done so in the past, policy and practice
was to avoid compulsory redundancy wherever possible in favour of staff
redeployment. Even the hybrid colleges are constrained by such policies,
though no formal power exists. One college, for example, deferred to the
authority's view on a particular staff matter, even though it formally would have
been free to act independently.

The fact that in maintained institutions the ultimate responsibility for
financial matters resides with the LEA means that they have to follow many
LEA procedures, and this has led to frequent claims of unnecessary interference in
matters in which the authorities lack expertise and which hampered the institutions' abilities to respond to constraint. This occurred in a variety of ways.

Preparation of budgets and control of expenditure

Normal practice is for estimates to be compiled within the institutions initially by the finance officer on behalf of the director but then scrutinized by the relevant sub-committee of the governing body before being passed to the academic board for scrutiny and comment. The wide variations in the level of detail contained within the estimates which we recorded earlier meant that different institutions had widely differing scopes for manoeuvre: the fewer heads, the greater flexibility. In one case the number of expenditure heads has been progressively reduced to increase flexibility in the subsequent use of permitted expenditure by avoiding the need for continual reference back for approval of allocation of funds to various heads; the institution's estimates now show fewer heads than the articles prescribe. In other cases *virement* between headings is seldom available and can only be obtained by approval of the relevant LEA committee. In all cases approval of estimates is required from the LEA, although the level of detailed scrutiny and amendment of estimates varies considerably. In some instances the LEA expects its own nominees on the governing body to exercise this function, whereas in other cases detailed scrutiny is undertaken by the relevant LEA committee.

Because our study has been principally concerned with the impact of financial constraint we investigated the procedures developed to scrutinize and when necessary reduce planned expenditure prior to the presentation of estimates. The most common action which has been taken in this respect has been the strengthening of finance office staff. Somewhat surprisingly we discovered that until quite recently the senior member of the finance office staff in more than one of our case studies was not a qualified accountant and exercised little more than a book-keeping role. Most of our case study institutions now employ qualified accountants who report directly to a member of the directorate, and are identified within the institutions as an integral part of the management team. This has the advantage not only of increasing the expertise within the institution but also of providing a focal point for communication between the LEA and the institution on financial matters. In particular better understanding of the financial problems of the institutions on the part of the LEA treasurers has proved useful in areas such as the level of topping up.

At the other extreme we have encountered instances where an LEA has forced expenditure on to an institution it maintains. One institution concerned operates over a number of dispersed sites but due to financial constraint in recent years has attempted to reduce the number of buildings from which it operates. This process has resulted in one relatively large building, which is a considerable distance from the major sites of the institution concerned, being only partially occupied and then only by administrative staff. Because 97 per cent of rents were, at the time of the study, chargeable to an open pool the LEA concerned requires the institution to continue with this presence despite the fact that vacating the site would lead to substantial savings to the institution. In another case, the polytechnic is unable to vacate a site because the LEA will not relinquish the lease before the due date.

Staffing

Both the Weaver and the Oakes reports advocated that broad control of expenditure on staffing by LEAs should be exercised through the budget preparation and scrutiny process. Although this recommendation has been accepted by the LEAs maintaining all of our case study institutions in respect of academic staff, there are wide differences in the mechanisms for controlling numbers and costs of non-academic staff. All our institutions are formally free to determine non-academic staff establishments within approved estimates, but various procedures are employed by maintaining authorities to impose non-academic staffing establishments. While these procedures are designed to achieve a measure of comparability between various categories of LEA employees, one of their effects is to remove discretion from institutions' managers in decisions on creation and grading of posts. This situation can, and indeed has, led to disputes between LEAs and the institutions they maintain. For example, in one case study institution where senior officers and management were generally appreciative of the support and relative operational independence granted by the LEA, the procedure for obtaining approval for posts and proposed grading commonly results in a 3-month delay between internal approval being given for the creation of a post and its subsequent advertisement. In another institution we were informed of frequent disagreement over both the creation and grading of posts. Since many such appointments are short-term, such delays can undermine the purpose of creating the post. In extreme cases LEAs can simply reject a proposal for the creation of a post although more frequently problems arise over gradings. On more than one occasion, senior institutional officers claimed that the relatively limited opportunities for career advancement within public sector higher education as compared to local government make it necessary to offer enhanced grading in order to attract applicants of sufficient quality. The LEA may then feel compelled to intervene in what is regarded within the institution as essentially an internal decision. For their part LEA officers have expressed a fear of a leap-frogging effect between salaries of authority and institutionally based staff and never-ending salary comparability disputes.

Contracts and purchases

Despite the fact that both the Weaver and Oakes reports, as well as the model articles of government contained in Circular 7/70, recommended that considerable discretion be granted to governing bodies in placing contracts and obtaining services, such discretion as we saw earlier is frequently limited and occasionally not available.

Some LEAs demand that institutions make use of their services, including the use of a Direct Labour Organization (DLO) for repairs and maintenance work. This may have advantages as was the case in more than one of our case study institutions, provided that the service is efficiently administered and delivered, in terms of flexibility of response to changing circumstances, avoidance of having staff idle during troughs in workload, avoidance of the need for complex supervisory and administrative systems which an in-house service would require and, in similar vein, avoidance of the risk of demarcation and other types of dispute.

A number of institutions, however, emphasized the disadvantages of an LEA providing repairs and maintenance services. In some instances this was argued on the basis of inefficiency in service delivery, in others on loss of control of decisions and resources. This latter point was illustrated at one split site institution which, due to a past merger, found itself with an LEA service at one site and an in-house service at another. The officer responsible for the in-house service argued that due to proper organization and planning it was possible to provide an efficient service and contain costs in a way which was not possible with LEA service delivery. In effect his argument was that it was 'too easy' to call in LEA services which had led to a loss of control over costs.

Similar arguments were put forward concerning the purchasing of goods and other services and similar variations were found in LEA policies. In some instances all purchases were required to be placed through a central supplies division or similar agency of the authority, while in others institutional managers retained wide discretion. In many cases the operation of the LEA procedures operated efficiently and the purchasing power of local authorities is such as to permit discounts to be obtained and substantial financial benefits to be passed on to the institutions. Where problems are encountered they normally related to inefficiency in authority systems or to what might be described as a lack of sensitivity to the operational needs of the institutions. In one case a local authority ordered the wrong equipment for its polytechnic and further expense was required in order to modify a building in which the equipment was to be stored. In another, a local authority audit of a library service reported that a proportion of the library stock had never been issued. This was taken to indicate that unnecessary stock was being carried and therefore the book fund could be cut. An intervention of the director was required to point out that much of the library stock was held for reference purposes only.

An area which has recently attracted a good deal of concern within some of our case study institutions has been the charging policies operated by their maintaining authorities particularly in respect of Central Establishment Charges levied by LEAs in respect of services such as audit, legal services, payroll, etc. The level, standard and type of services provided can and do vary widely from one institution to another, as do the charges levied. This raises particular problems for institutional managers for whom no formal channels are available to enable challenges to be entered in respect of these charges. In response to financial constraint, in two case study institutions it was decided during 1984–5 to request from the LEAs details of their calculations. In neither case were institutional managers satisfied with the responses to these requests. While these charges are not a major element of institutional costs, they represent an area in which institutional managers are normally unable to achieve economies. Not only does this undermine attempts to improve institutions' financial efficiency but frequently serves to sour the relationship between the LEAs and the institutions.

7.4 Conclusions

There was a great deal of diversity in the policies, procedures and practises of local authorities and their impact on maintained and 'hybrid' institutions, but we can identify a number of areas of continuing concern regarding the impact of LEA involvement in institutional management. On the positive side, our case studies showed that a number of LEAs adopt supportive roles towards their institutions, provide a range of important services through the technical and professional expertise of their staff and, in some cases, effectively subsidize their institutions through, for example, charging for services on a marginal cost basis or lower, or meeting part of rate costs. Our institutions benefited from this support in times of stringency, in particular when the authority was able to act as a buffer when AFE Pool funds were reduced.

In other cases the involvement of LEAs in institutional management varied between a source of irritation and outright direct control. In these cases institutions tended to report that the authorities' policies and procedures hampered their flexibility in responding to constraint. Institutions, too, reported problems of general local authority policies on such matters as compulsory redundancy hampering their freedom to manoeuvre, though we sometimes felt that these constraints were covertly welcomed as they precluded institutions from taking unpleasant options.

Despite the examples of successful relationships between local authorities and institutions we are bound to conclude from the evidence of the others that the original formulation of the framework of college and polytechnic governance, drawing as it did on the university and direct grant models of independent institutions, had not been consistently successfully applied in the public sector. The success or failure of the devolved model of institutional management too often crucialy depended on the goodwill of those within the maintaining authorities responsible for general oversight of the institutions. There had been considerable time for the Weaver principles to be implemented and accepted by the authorities, and our findings of their failure, albeit partial, confirm a need for reform.

Such reform, of course, is now taking place following the 1987 White Paper on higher education (DES 1987). The major public sector colleges are to be given independent corporate status and funded centrally. Their constitutional links with the local authorities will be severed, ending the separate public sector of higher education under the control of democratically elected bodies. Corporate status may give the maintained institutions the freedom they believe they need, but it is beyond the scope of this book to discuss the implications in detail, though we comment on some points in Chapter 8. Locke *et al.* (1987) present the issues for polytechnics and consider alternatives. Our own view is that the government need not have chosen this, the most drastic option. It could have considered a comprehensive review of the operation of the existing system, in order to provide unambiguous criteria governing the relationship between institutions and authorities, and establishing machinery to make sure that any redefinition of the relationship was properly enforced. Alternatively, the generally favourable experience of one of our 'hybrid' colleges, in its more independent relationship with its local authority as well as illustrating what might have been possible had the spirit of Weaver pervaded authorities, suggests that a more fruitful model of institutional governance might be developed. The shared responsibility of the college between its trustee governors and the authority shows that it is possible for independent institutions to work fruitfully with a local authority and yet retain sufficient independence to respond to constraint.

References

Council for Local Education Authorities (1981) Draft Report of the Review Group on College Government: Unpublished paper prepared by CLEA and officials of the DES.

Department of Education and Science (1987) *Higher Education: Meeting the Challenge.* Cmnd 114. London: HMSO.

Education Science and Arts Committee (1980) *The Funding and Organisation of Courses in Higher Education.* London: HMSO.

Locke, M. (1974) Government. In Pratt, J. and Burgess, T. (eds) *Polytechnics: A Report.* London: Pitman.

Locke, M., Pratt, J., Silverman, S. and Travers, T. (1987) *Polytechnic Government: A Report Commissioned by the Committee of Directors of Polytechnics.* CDP.

Oakes, G. (1978) *Report of the Working Group on the Management of Higher Education in the Maintained Sector.* Cmnd 7130. London: HMSO.

Weaver Report (1966) *Report of the Study Group on The Government of Colleges of Education.* London: HMSO.

8

Conclusions

This book has examined a major departure in British public administration – the central planning and control of the public sector of higher education through the 1984–5 planning exercise of the National Advisory Body. It has recorded and analysed the management responses to constraint of eight case study institutions, and some of the factors that affected them. These responses have a number of implications and consequences, not all of which were anticipated either by institutions or the government and NAB. In this chapter, we first summarize our findings and then go on to examine some of these unintended consequences and their implications for public policy-making. We conclude by suggesting some measures to improve policy-making for education in the future.

8.1 Findings

Although the establishment of NAB meant a uniform, centrally administered instrument was used to distribute student numbers and AFE Pool funds, we found that it had widely differing effects and consequences. For some institutions, it meant a continuation of a series of cuts since the AFE Pool was capped; for others it meant increased resources; for some, hoped-for benefits did not arrive. While it may have been a *national* planning exercise, for many institutions it inhibited, precluded or negated institutional planning.

A critical factor explaining these differences in institutional impacts was the different circumstances in which institutions found themselves as a result of their previous histories. Although they were undergoing the same national exercise, institutions faced quite different problems, and there is therefore no single pattern of overall response that can be said to be 'good' or 'bad' practice, or to conform with government policy. Decisions taken as much as 15 years ago, at the time of the formation of the institutions, still affected the options open to managers in 1984–5: some institutions which had a history of cuts before the NAB exercise had already learned lessons on how to cope with sudden changes in financial circumstances and developed flexible institutional strategies. Other institutions were still coping with the effects of recent mergers or other local circumstances which limited their freedom of manoeuvre in response to financial constraint.

Common features

Despite these differences, however, we can identify some common features in the pattern of policies adopted by our case study institutions. These included a tendency to preserve academic profiles despite reductions in resources, an emphasis on reorganizing academic structures and processes, an emphasis on improving procedures for monitoring and evaluation of courses, a tendency to seek improvements in institutional status, and perhaps most significant of all, an emphasis on measures to improve 'efficiency'. Institutional managers felt they could not afford to ignore government imperatives to move toward 'efficiency' as defined by indicators such as SSRs, and they responded sooner or later by maintaining (or often increasing) student numbers at lower unit costs. In short they opted for what we describe as the 'efficiency option'. In this regard, we see the responses to the NAB exercise as a continuation of a trend over a number of years rather than as a one-off response to a crisis.

The efficiency option

In adopting the 'efficiency option' our institutions were behaving in a way that many studies of organizations have described. These show that it is easier for organizations and managers within them to respond to constraint conserva- tively, by cutting costs rather than radically reappraising their products, func- tions or services. When it examined British universities, the Jarratt Committee commented unfavourably on their lack of strategic planning and coordination between academic planning and resource allocation (CVCP 1985), and their findings confirmed those of Shattock and Rigby (1983).

In line with these findings, few of our institutions sought to make radical reappraisals of their objectives and functions. They did not produce the kind of strategic plan or mission statement or undergo the processes of 'portfolio analysis' recommended in the copious literature on this subject (e.g. Sizer 1982). Few managers found the NAB planning exercise a satisfactory environ- ment in which to develop such plans. Instead there was a tendency to crisis management, directly related to the limited planning horizons caused by shifts in government policy and uncertainties about their future financial situation.

Institutions facing large cuts could do little else than get spending within acceptable levels, and since the time-scale for the exercise was short, there was little time for detailed planning in these circumstances. Moreover, the annual change in the ways in which the AFE Pool had been allocated since it was capped meant that it tended to favour one kind of institution or one type of activity rather than another on different occasions, though institutions could not be sure of exactly how until close to the beginning of the financial year. The sense of aiming at a moving target was heightened during the planning exercise by the widely discussed alternative ways of allocating the pool between the indicative allocation in August and the final allocation in December 1983. As O'Hara has shown (1985), the implementation of some of the alternatives would have significantly altered the allocations received by institutions. As it was, even institutions which prioritized in response to the planning exercise reported (confirming Davies and Morgan's, 1982, findings) a sense of unreality about the exercise, and staff did not believe that actual institutional allocations would have been made according to these plans.

Resource allocation and control

The felt need to adopt the 'efficiency option' and to increase control over resources involved changes to existing procedures or the development of new ones in most of our case study institutions. Institutions which were already operating at high SSRs generally had such systems; others found they had to be created quickly. Much of the literature on responses to constraint is concerned with the extent to which such systems should or must inevitably be centralized. Shattock and Rigby (1983), in their study of British universities, found not only that some of their institutions chose to avoid such centralization of decision-making but argued that those which did centralize may not have dealt so successfully with cuts as those which did not. In most of our cases the intention and effect was to heighten control of resources and to centralize control. Even when a system used the participative procedures of academic governance members of the directorate became identified as the key figures determining staffing and often seemed pleased to be so regarded.

While our case study institutions made changes to their procedures, it is worth noting that few of them felt the need to establish special committees or new structures to cope with the problems of constraint in the NAB planning exercise. In this they differed somewhat from the universities. Shattock and Rigby (1983) found that their sample of British universities in the 1980s had a variety of structures for planning and resource allocation, and that institutions responded to constraint in different ways. Some moved towards more centralized control; some set up special emergency procedures with small, powerful committees to take difficult decisions; others sought more devolved control; another, while setting up a new committee to coordinate responses, sought to maintain its normal constitutional procedures.

In the public sector, our findings suggest that in response to the NAB planning exercise, there was less of a tendency to create special committees or new structures for planning and resource allocation than in the universities. Only one of our institutions set up a special committee to deal with prioritization. Most institutions sought to use their existing structures of academic governance and executive responsibility of directorates, though one attempted to introduce, and others began to consider, more devolved responsibility to cost centres. Even the one institution which substantially restructured as a response to constraint still used as far as possible its normal (reformed) structures to deal with the NAB exercise and continuing constraint.

In part these findings can be explained by noting some important differences between the university and public sectors. Local authority funding and, in the case of maintained institutions, formal responsibility for control of expenditure, meant that none of our institutions had the kind of 'block grant' allocation of funds for academic activities that is commonly made by university councils to their senates. Public sector institutions have always had to consider each head of spending in some detail, though the number of heads varies appreciably from institution to institution. As a consequence, and perhaps paradoxically, the differential treatment between academic and non-academic heads that Shattock and Rigby found in universities tends not to occur in public sector institutions. Where universities often allow non-academic spending to be dealt with by executive action of the relevant officers, these items are normally scrutinized by the same basic procedures as academic staffing items in the public sector.

Quality and efficiency

Another common feature of the pattern of policies adopted by our case study institutions was an emphasis on improving academic quality by tightening up procedures for the monitoring and evaluation of courses. These procedural changes were often related to their changing relationship with the CNAA and in many of our institutions with aspirations for higher status.

The desire of colleges to become polytechnics or polytechnics to become universities is obviously related to the improved funding opportunities seen for institutions at the higher levels. One unanticipated consequence of such aspirations, however, was an identification of quality with higher-level courses and research rather than excellence in teaching or course development. When combined with the tendency to take the efficiency option, this emphasis can mean that institutional policies pushed academic staffs' increasingly restricted time for development toward the goal of research or work on higher-level courses rather than in developing new teaching methods or course structures to cope with the larger classes often caused by higher SSRs. Improving quality was thus defined in these relatively narrow terms.

There were other implications for quality, too, in the responses to the planning exercise. Because institutions felt obliged to respond to the 'efficiency' imperatives of the exercise by attempting to control expenditure and increasing their SSRs, they increasingly made use of the NAB/HMI best-practice SSRs in the allocation and control of resources to courses. In part they did so for reasons that Fielden (1982) has outlined. He argues that participative groups (like higher education institutions) find it difficult to agree on the quality of competing bids and 'tend to welcome such quantitative aids which can be accepted as fair to all'. Public sector institutions have used NAB SSR weightings in exactly this fashion to make difficult decisions about overstaffing and possible redundancy as well as resource allocation to courses.

Our findings show, however, that standard indicators, based as they often are on notional calculations, are unable to take account of actual differences between institutions, subject areas, etc. As a result, institutions or courses which do not conform to the 'national' pattern for whatever reason can be penalized. For example, innovative courses structured on a multi-disciplinary or modular basis suffered from the categorization of courses into NAB's strict programme areas. Courses which by their nature required small group teaching, such as practical 'hands-on' training with expensive equipment, in-service education requiring intensive visiting, clinical work or fieldwork, were all threatened by higher SSRs. The weighting system adopted by the DES for part-time work was seen to threaten its viability in some institutions.

The potential for innovation was further threatened by the increasing emphasis on higher SSRs, since work by staff to develop new teaching methods or adapt course structures to deal with bigger classes was precisely the kind of activity threatened by the time limitations imposed by higher SSRs. While actual contact time may not go up with bigger classes, the 'iceberg effect' of more marking and course preparation was reported by teaching staff in many institutions. These kind of unintended consequences of adopting a definition of efficiency in terms of standard SSRs were not always discussed in the bodies responsible for planning in our case study institutions.

8.2 Policy and outcomes

As we made clear in Chapters 1 and 4, we see this book as a test of the policies of the government and NAB at the time of the planning exercise, as well of the institutions' responses to the circumstances in which the policies and actions of these agencies placed them.

A central concern of government education policy in the period covered by this study was the need to reduce expenditure. This derived in large part from the adverse economic circumstances that affected the UK as well as most of the Western world, but in this country was intensified by a clear policy view that public expenditure needed to be constrained to enhance the opportunity for the private sector of the economy to develop. In the public sector of higher education in particular, spending was held to be out of control because of the 'pool' system of funding. Added to these issues was continuing concern that higher education should relate more closely with the needs of the economy and the labour market. All these longstanding problems, each reinforcing the urgency of the others, together created circumstances in which the creation of a central planning body and the NAB planning exercise appeared to be inevitable. In the planning exercise, as we saw in Chapter 3, NAB attempted to tackle several problems – reducing resources, maintaining access and quality, geographical balance of provision and giving priority to scientific and technological provision of relevance to industry.

To the extent that institutions took actions to improve their efficiency and take account of government priorities, it might be said that these aspects of government policy were successfully implemented through the planning exercise, and there was undoubtedly a shift in course provision across the country towards science and technology. But were the consequences of taking the 'efficiency option' in line with the intentions of policy-makers? In particular, were institutions able to maintain the quality of their courses as well as access to them? Was the NAB exercise set up in such a way as to allow them to plan strategically to deal with the consequences of adopting such a policy?

When we examine the consequences of taking the 'efficiency option', it seems clear that the implementation of the NAB exercise did not carry out the intentions of policy-makers to reduce expenditure while maintaining access and quality. Because of the way both 'efficiency' and 'quality' were defined, institutional policies threatened the innovative character of some courses and access to courses by some students, such as part-timers. This failure can be attributed, at least in part, to unrealistic assumptions on the part of policy-makers and their failure to put institutions in a situation, the logic of which, would encourage managers to plan strategically and make difficult decisions about the long-term character of their institutions. It can also be attributed, however, to the tendency of institutional managers to import outside indicators into internal resource allocation procedures without examining the consequences of such policies or relating academic planning to a sense of the overall aims or 'mission' of the institution.

There is agreement among many analysts that policy-making in a period of financial constraint differs significantly from its characteristics under growth conditions. As William Boyd (1983) puts it:

> there is a fundamental shift from distributive to redistributive politics; a shrinking budget creates clear winners and losers, and no slack resources remain with which to buy off the losers with side payments on secondary issues.

Boyd contends that in a period of decline, resource allocation decisions become more difficult, participation is intensified, decisions are complicated by considerations of equity and entitlement and morale plummets in declining organizations.

The central question of management in a period of financial constraint is who will bear the immediate and long-term costs of cutbacks. Behn (1980) has argued that there are two fundamental stages in retrenchment, the first concerned with short-run, across the board cuts which minimize conflict and defer difficult decisions. But managers must eventually face up to the second stage, which involves concentrated cuts designed to protect the long-term interests of the organization. Behn argues that it is in the interests of managers to get past the first stage as quickly as possible by making clear the opportunity costs of not cutting back and the specific consequences for the organization. He proposes that leaders should articulate a new 'corporate strategy' or organization mission that shows who will benefit by the transformation and contraction of the organization.

Mission statements

When 'mission statements' are discussed, many people think this means a detailed elaborate document outlining everything the institution will do for the next 10 years or more. The turbulent environment, however, militates against such exact predictions and we are arguing that 'mission' should mean a sense of the problems they are trying to solve, rather than a listing of the activities that they currently or propose to undertake. The institutions should see themselves as solutions to problems, which are located in the environment of the institution – locally, regionally and nationally. Mission statements should first be in terms of these problems which institutions are trying to solve, and second discussing the solutions which are proposed to tackle them. In different circumstances, different solutions may be appropriate or necessary, because new constraints may rule some out or allow previously rejected solutions to be adopted. If mission statements are simply based on an institution's activities, rather than the goals of such activities, then the institution will react to constraint by trying to preserve as many of these activities as possible – the kind of conservative reaction we have seen – rather than by flexibly anticipating changes in the environment.

If this kind of mission statement is discussed democratically throughout the institution, then strategies developed to deal with financial constraint are more likely to generate consensus. Bodies responsible for planning will be able to evaluate policies on the basis of these agreed goals and they can provide the necessary forum for a discussion of the consequences of changing institutional strategies. Mission statements are good practice only if they are in terms of solutions to problems and are democratically adopted by the institution as a whole. They can then allow the appropriate planning bodies to evaluate institutional strategies and ensure that the institution is moving in the direction in which it wishes to move.

Strategic planning under constraint is difficult for any organization, but the parameters of the NAB planning exercise did not encourage institutions to look at long-term goals because planning horizons were short and the rules of the game were constantly changing. We would agree with the Jarratt Committee from the findings of our study that institutions need a clear indication from government of the broad objectives of the system so that they can operate with reasonable foresight. As it was, even institutions which did anticipate the nature of the NAB exercise sometimes found their foresight was a mixed blessing. The policy of 'turning up the burner' at one institution meant that, in its view, it received a lower Pool allocation than it should have done because other institutions had not been so efficient and the allocations had to be 'damped' to cope with these institutions. Being too far ahead of the field can be almost as bad as being too far behind in a system which is designed to achieve uniformity.

The logic of the situation in which institutions found themselves was also influenced by their local environments. As we saw in Chapter 7, while many institutions had supportive relationships with their local authorities, their freedom of action was also clearly limited either as a direct result of their instruments and articles of government or because of particular local authority policies or practices. For example, in the first category was the institutions' inability to carry forward any surplus funds into the next financial year, which restricts their ability to take an entrepreneurial role. In the second category were the authority's policy on redundancy or the institution's lack of control of certain areas of expenditure, such as central establishment charges. The inability of more than one of our case study institutions to move out of buildings which were considered unsatisfactory points to the kind of problems arising from local constraints which faced institutions' managers trying to control expenditure and cope with cuts in funding.

8.3   Creating an environment for management

The combination of national and local constraints meant that institutions' freedom of action was restricted and the logic of their situations did not encourage the kind of long-term planning needed to cope with financial constraint. If national bodies expect institutions to engage in strategic planning, they must not only provide stable planning horizons, but recognize that institutions need freedom to manoeuvre in order to develop local initiatives and respond to local circumstances. Controls from the centre must recognize that there are differences between institutions and that institutions with clear goals should be rewarded. They cannot expect institutions to take innovative measures if such initiatives mean that the institutions are penalized in their future funding. Central goals and priorities should not totally supplant local initiatives. Furthermore, local authorities should see that limits imposed on the institutions' freedom of action can also stifle innovation and prevent them from developing the best strategy to cope with financial constraint.

Policy-making under adversity

In his most recent work, Dror (1986) describes how governments tend to react in periods of adversity. What he calls 'primary response patterns' include a tendency to denial and simplification, attempts to externalize or transfer the problem, and to maintain that basic assumptions need not be altered. At the same time, faced with the complex, intractable and apparently insoluble problems of adversity they feel a need to act, sometimes embarking on a 'policy-making stampede'; often they attempt to relocate responsibilities, sometimes by devolution, sometimes involving centralization. They attempt to reduce public expectations, and may blame the problem on moral degeneration or external forces. While all these responses are taking place, they usually continue with the traditional incremental patterns of policy-making, demonstrating a tendency

> not to think in the correct order of magnitude. But eventually, as adversity becomes manifest and incrementalism clearly inadequate a number of sporadic jumps in policies enter the response pattern . . . as a semiconvulsive response to overwhelming stimuli that have been permitted to build up for a long time without treatment. (Dror 1986, p. 57)

When we analyse the actions of the government in creating NAB and the establishment of the 1984–5 planning exercise, we can see many elements of this familiar pattern of response. The creation of NAB was a reallocation of responsibility and involved unprecedented centralization; the need to externalize and transfer the problem can be traced in the attitude of the government which wanted to reduce expenditure on higher education yet still expected it to maintain access and quality. NAB in turn transferred many of the problems to institutions, yet limited their freedom of action to respond effectively.

The NAB exercise was designed, at least in part, to use the new mechanisms of central control to put pressure on institutions to reduce expenditure by being more 'efficient' in government terms. Policy-makers were able to decide on a policy of reducing expenditure while maintaining access and quality only by assuming that there was room for improvements in efficiency on the part of institutions which would allow such cuts to be made. Whether such an assumption was warranted was left to institutional managers to discover, although the government did have to consider alternative hypotheses. For example, the government's decision to put an additional £20 m into the AFE Pool in October 1983 was seen as an acknowledgment of NAB's contention that lowering the unit of resource would have a serious impact on access.

NAB transferred the problem to the institutions while still having an important role in setting limits to their freedom of action. As we saw in Chapter 3, NAB was faced with a series of conflicting priorities, some coming from the DES and others from members of its board, which included representatives from local authorities, teachers unions, etc. Rather than acting simply as 'implementer' of government policy, NAB became part of the policy-making process itself. NAB was designed, at least to some extent, to act as a buffer between higher education institutions and the government. In this role, it struggled to arrive at a reasonable distribution of the AFE Pool, taking into account the many conflicting priorities which it had to resolve.

NAB implemented government policy by making it clear that its funding methodology was designed to reward the 'efficient' institutions, but it still maintained that decisions about resource allocation were up to institutional managers. Despite NAB's contention that institutions were free to manage their budgets as they saw fit, it was difficult for managers to see AFE funding as a 'black box' and spend their Pool allocation according to their own internal priorities. The penalty for such a strategy was the strong possibility of receiving a smaller allocation the next year, which was understandably hard for managers to see as a successful strategy.

8.4 Postscript: Independence for the public sector

NAB was able to learn many lessons from the experience of the 1984–5 planning exercise, some of which were evident in the second exercise it conducted for 1987–8. This exercise, for example, gave institutions a somewhat longer timetable in which to consider and submit their plans; prioritization on the lines of the 1984–5 exercise was abandoned. The sub-quantum method of funding was dropped. But some lessons – such as the reduction of complexity in funding – still seem to have to be learned. The number of programme areas increased; the formulae and calculation of units of resource remain as complex as ever, and they differ yet again from those employed in 1984–5. But there now seems little likelihood that NAB will be able to put its experience and the lessons of the 1984–5 or the 1987–8 planning exercises into practice – even if it wanted to. For it will soon go out of existence. The White Paper on Higher Education in April 1987 announced the government's intention to give independent status to polytechnics and major colleges in the public sector, and to abolish NAB (DES 1987).

The White Paper marks an increase in the central control of higher education; for both the university and public sectors, new bodies will be created to control the planning and funding of institutions. For the public sector, the White Paper announced that institutions would achieve independent corporate status and no longer have direct LEA links, but be funded from central government via a Polytechnics and Colleges Funding Council (PCFC), with a strong non-academic membership. The PCFC would allocate its funds on the basis of 'contracts' with the institutions rather than as grants. The changes are intended to enable the system to 'serve the economy more effectively' and 'have closer links with industry and commerce and promote enterprise', and the White Paper emphasizes the need to improve 'efficiency'. The system of contracts for funding is to encourage institutions to be 'enterprising' in attracting contracts from other sources, to lessen their reliance on public funds, to sharpen accountability and strengthen their commitment to the delivery of the educational services they have agreed with the funding body.

The extent of change proposed by the government took most people in the British higher education system by surprise. Most had expected the institutions to be given a measure of independence from the local authorities: few, however, anticipated their removal from local authority involvement altogether. This marks the virtual end of a century of local authority involvement in higher education, and we wonder if institutional managers will benefit as much as they think in exchanging the admittedly often irksome controls of local authorities for a more direct relationship with central government. The White Paper's proposals for 'contract' funding, too, went further than most people expected and caused widespread concern in institutions, as did similar proposals for the universities. The abolition of NAB was also something of a surprise. It means that it had barely 5 years existence before its demise was announced. It would not be difficult to characterize this decision in Dror's terms, as one of the 'semi-convulsive' responses to stimuli that have been allowed to build up over a long period of time.

We cannot detail here the many problems and issues that these developments will raise for the institutions, the government and the new PCFC. We can, however, reflect briefly on what lessons there are from the study we have conducted for the operation of the new independent colleges under a PCFC.

One comment we can make in the light of the study of the 1984–5 NAB planning exercise concerns the process and time-scale of change. Many of the difficulties that the NAB faced in its planning exercise and those that it created for institutions were of kinds familiar in the analysis of public policy-making. In the terminology used by Simon (1960), most of the decision- and policy-making by NAB, government and institutions was 'non-programmed'. There were at the outset no specific procedures for dealing with the situation and the actors had to 'fall back on whatever general capacity (they had) for intelligent, adaptive, problem oriented action'. NAB had to make up the rules of the game as it went along, because – in part at least – the rules and objectives set for it by government were changing. In turn this placed institutions in circumstances in which it was difficult to plan ahead. While it is true that NAB was trying to create a 'programmed' framework in the planning exercise through the analysis of options and alternatives, the general experience was very much one of Lindblom's 'muddling through'. The prospects for the institutions and the PCFC, at least in its early years, are that it will be 'more of the same'. The PCFC is to take responsibility from 1 April 1989, just under 2 years from the date of the White Paper. At the time of writing it is not yet established, which means that it will have even less time to prepare for its task than NAB had between *its* establishment and the start of the financial year 1984–5.

The NAB exercise showed that what is needed in planning public sector higher education is a much more *systematic* process in which institutions can plan their futures within a national context; that is, as Simon advocates, the extension of programmed decision-making into unprogrammed areas so far as possible. The key to developing a process of systematic change lies in returning to the notion we set out in Chapter 1, of taking a problem-solving approach to public policy and institutions, and in identifying an apt allocation of responsibility – clarifying who should be responsible for what within the system – and also more importantly, perhaps, what they should *not* be responsible for. In the context of a policy to increase central control this becomes more important than ever.

There is little denying that central government has a function, reflected in the law, in formulating the overall national problems to which higher education is seen as a solution – what Kogan and Boys (1982) call 'framework decisions' – as well as determining the total amount of money to be spent on this and of ensuring that its expenditure is controlled. But this does not mean it should itself control the spending or its detailed distribution.

There is the obvious danger that the centre may get the national needs wrong. There is considerable evidence of that in the history of attempts at manpower planning, for example, and the government has itself acknowledged these difficulties (Carlisle 1979). The centralist approach assumes an omniscience that in practice (and probably in principle, too) is unattainable. A second danger is that the centre will set out for its institutions detailed prescriptions of what they ought to do. James (1980) has called this 'solutioneering' – the tendency to propose solutions without being clear what the problem is. We would add that solutioneering usually also involves the centre prescribing solutions that it is not competent to do. It is implausible that a part-time committee even with a professional secretariat, however knowledgeable they may be, can determine, as NAB attempted to do, what courses should be run in all the multifarious subject areas in all the colleges in the public sector. A third danger is that the centre will impose on institutions substantial and possibly unmanageable changes whenever it takes a new view of national needs. It is not hard to describe the 1984–5 NAB planning exercise in these terms.

These considerations and the experience of the 1984–5 NAB planning exercise suggest that there is a need to delineate and limit the role of any central planning and funding body to tasks it can tackle reasonably. Considering institutions as attempts to solve some problem or problems offers a way of doing this. The task of PCFC should be restricted to formulating the national problems to which the public sector is to offer its solutions, and judging the proposals from and funding the institutions whose proposals seem most likely to succeed in tackling those problems. PCFC cannot, of its nature, prescribe the educational solutions. That is the task for the institutions.

For PCFC to carry out this task would involve some significant changes from the mode of operation adopted by NAB in the 1984–5 planning exercise. It would have first to offer a formulation of national problems. This would need to be made before any planning exercise took place, and not part way through as in the 1984–5 planning exercise. This is no mean task, which is perhaps why it is rarely done. It is alarming how difficult it is to find an overall view of the state of the nation and the direction in which it is desired to go. It would be important in the context of the White Paper that the formulation includes a statement of all the kinds of overall problems that PSHE might tackle. The White Paper's concern with the needs of the economy should not obscure the importance of wider aims and functions of higher education.

The basis for such a formulation already exists in the statement that NAB made with the UGC (1984). The statement might contain a kind of 'national scenario' like that suggested by Sizer (1982). This might include present and anticipated economic development at national, regional and sectoral levels, with comparable data on employment, investment, developments in public services, known and anticipated labour and skills shortages, etc. But while this statement should outline problems – in the sense of stating where we are now and where we wish to be – it is emphatically *not* a forecast of what will happen, nor will it prescribe solutions to the problems. Thus while it might describe manpower shortages (when these can be authenticated), it would not prescribe the output of colleges that would be required to meet them; there may be other ways of solving the problem.

A major component of any statement would be PCFC's priorities, again identified before institutions produce their responses, which might be reflected in its broad allocation of funds by what one of us (Pratt 1982) has called 'problem budgeting'. PCFC would indicate which problems it regarded as most important, and indicate the levels of resources it anticipated devoting to their solution. The important point here is that resource allocation is related to the importance of the problem. Included in the statement would be the criteria to be employed in considering proposals from institutions or authorities. They may include such criteria as 'cost-effectiveness' and might recognize such criteria as 'educational value added'.

It follows from this approach that, in judging proposals for contract funding, PCFC would take what might be termed an 'investment model' approach, behaving rather like institutional investors in the private sector when considering a proposal from a company. It would regard its funds as an investment, not a subvention, and require the institution to explain why it should invest in the institution; the onus would be on the institution to satisfy it on its likely success. PCFC's role would be restricted to 'investment appraisal'; it would not concern itself in any detail with the institutions' 'production processes'.

The experience of the NAB planning exercise suggests that proposals from institutions, which would be the basis of any PCFC contract, should relate financial and numerical plans with academic purposes, and should be set in a reasonable time horizon for development. The proposals would thus take the form of costed academic development plans, for say 3 years ahead, not just a statistical return. They would cover all kinds of educational activity, research as well as teaching. They would set out the institution's response to the 'national scenario'. They might propose an alternative scenario. The character of an institution and the education it offered would be seen as an attempt to tackle problems identified and would be justified in these terms, and amplified where appropriate by more local information. The plans would be proposed, considered and funded as a whole. PCFC cannot realistically add a few more engineers here, cut a dozen sociologists there. The proposals would be judged by PCFC in the light of its published criteria; it would be up to PCFC to ensure that the overall distribution of funds to different kinds of activity reflected its problem budget.

The experience of the NAB planning exercise suggests that PCFC will need to establish mechanisms of monitoring the effects of its own actions, and of finding ways of assessing how far what happens in colleges addresses the problems it has identified. This is not just a matter of establishing whether or not changes in the pattern of provision have taken place, but also of devising ways of assessing whether or not these changes, and hence PCFC's activities, are helping to solve the problems of individuals and the nation as a whole through education. For this study has confirmed repeated findings in the history of further education in England (e.g. Locke *et al.* 1986) that colleges respond to the logic of their situations, rather than in a spirit of obedience to government policy or of 'common interest'. They seek to maximize benefits to themselves. They seek resources, prestige, status, and students, and they endeavour to exploit the administrative measures, methods of allocating funds, etc. to their own advantage. They respond to the constraints and opportunities of their environments, environments in which PCFC itself will be a major component and which it can affect to a considerable extent. PCFC will need to consider how far the environment offers to institutional managers the scope to make reasonable plans for their futures and to staff the incentives to make themselves more cost-effective. This study has shown how great is the need for such an environment.

References

Behn, R. (1980) Leadership for Cut-back Management: The Use of Corporate Strategy. *Public Administration Review*, 40, pp. 613–20.

Boyd. W. L. (1983) Rethinking Educational Policy and Management: Political Science and Educational Administration in the 1980s. *American Journal of Education*, November, pp. 1–29.

Carlisle, M. (1979) Letter to Education, Arts and Science Committee of the House of Commons, 13 December.

Committee of Vice Chancellors and Principals (CVCP) (1985) *Report of the Steering Committee for Efficiency Studies in Universities*. CVCP.

Davies, J. L. and Morgan A. W. (1982) The Politics of Institutional Change. In Wagner, L. (ed.) *Agenda for Institutional Change in Higher Education*. Guildford: SRHE.

Department of Education and Science (1987) *Higher Education: Meeting the Challenge*. Cmnd 114. London: HMSO.

Dror, Y. (1986) *Policymaking Under Adversity*. New Brunswick: Transaction.

Fielden, J. (1982) Strategies for Survival. In Morris, A. and Sizer, J. (eds) *Resources and Higher Education*. Guildford: SRHE.

James, R. (1980) *Return to Reason: Popper's Thought in Public Life*. Somerset: Open Books.

Kogan, M. and Boys, C. (1982) The Politics of Sectoral Change in Higher Education. In Wagner L. (ed.) *Agenda for Institutional Change in Higher Education*. Guildford: SRHE.

Locke, M., Pratt, J. and Burgess, T. (1986) *The Central Management of Organic Change: The Colleges of Higher Education 1972 to 1982*. Croydon: Critical Press.

National Advisory Body for Local Authority Higher Education/University Grants Committee (NAB/UGC) (1984) *Adapting to a Changing World*.

O'Hara, R. (1985) Avoiding the Unavoidable – Formula Funding and Institutional Costs in PSHE. CIS Commentary 29, North East London Polytechnic.

Pratt, J. (1982) Resource Allocation within one Public Sector. In Morris, A. and Sizer, J. (eds) *Resources and Higher Education*. Guildford: SRHE.

Shatlock, M. and Rigby, G. (1983) *Resources Allocation in British Universities*. Guildford: SRHE.

Simon, H. A. (1960) *The New Science of Management Decision*. Englewood Cliffs, N.J.: Prentice Hall.

Sizer, J. (1982) Assessing Institutional Performance and Progress. In Wagner, L. (ed.) *Agenda for Institutional Change in Higher Education*. Guildford: SRHE.

Index

The Society for Research into Higher Education

The Society exists both to encourage and co-ordinate research and development into all aspects of Higher Education, including academic, organizational and policy issues; and also to provide a forum for debate, verbal and printed. Through its activities, it draws attention to the significance of research into, and development in, Higher Education and to the needs of scholars in this field. (It is not concerned with research generally, except, for instance, as a subject of study.)

The Society's income derives from subscriptions, book sales, conferences and specific grants. It is wholly independent. Its corporate members are institutions of higher education, research institutions and professional, industrial, and governmental bodies. Its individual members include teachers and researchers, administrators and students. Members are found in all parts of the world and the Society regards its international work as amongst its most important activities.

The Society discusses and comments on policy, organizes conferences and encourages research. Under the Imprint SRHE & OPEN UNIVERSITY PRESS, it is a specialist publisher, having some 40 titles in print. It also publishes *Studies in Higher Education* (three times a year) which is mainly concerned with academic issues, *Higher Education Quarterly* (formerly *Universities Quarterly*) which will be mainly concerned with policy issues, *Research into Higher Education Abstracts* (three times a year), and a *Bulletin* (six times a year).

The Society's committees, study groups and branches are run by members (with help from a small staff at Guildford), and aim to provide a forum for discussion. The groups at present include a Teacher Education Study Group, a Staff Development Group, a Women in Higher Education Group and a Continuing Education Group which may have had their own organization, subscriptions or publications (e.g. the *Staff Development Newsletter*). The Governing Council, elected by members, comments on current issues; and discusses policies with leading figures, notably at its evening Forums. The Society organizes seminars on current research for officials of DES and other ministries, an Anglo-American series on standards, and is in touch with bodies in the UK such as the NAB, CVCP, UGC, CNAA and the British Council, and with sister-bodies overseas. Its current research projects include one on the relationship between entry qualifications and degree results, directed by Prof. W. D. Furneaux (Brunel) and one on questions of quality directed by Prof. G. C. Moodie (York). A project on the evaluation of the research standing of university departments is in preparation. The Society's conferences are often held jointly. Annual Conferences have considered 'Professional Education' (1984), 'Continuing Education' (1985, with Goldsmiths' College) 'Standards and Criteria in Higher Education' (1986, with Bulmershe CHE), 'Restructuring' (1987, with the City of Birmingham Polytechnic) and 'Academic Freedom' (1988, the University of

Surrey). Other conferences have considered the DES 'Green Paper' (1985, with the *Times Higher Education Supplement*), and 'The First-Year Experience' (1986, with the University of South Carolina and Newcastle Polytechnic). For some of the Society's conferences, special studies are commissioned in advance, as 'Precedings'.

Members receive free of charge the Society's *Abstracts*, annual conference Proceedings (or 'Precedings'), *Bulletin and International Newsletter* and may buy SRHE & OPEN UNIVERSITY PRESS books at booksellers' discount. Corporate members also receive the Society's journal *Studies in Higher Education* free (individuals at a heavy discount). They may also obtain *Evaluation Newsletter* and certain other journals at a discount, including the NFER *Register of Educational Research*. There is a substantial discount to members, and to staff of corporate members, on annual and some other conference fees.